Christian Witness
Among Muslims

Living Sacrifice Book Company
Bartlesville, OK 74003

Christian Witness Among Muslims

First published in 1971 by the African Christian Press, Box 30, Achimota, Ghana, Africa.

Published by Living Sacrifice Book Company, a division of The Voice of the Martyrs, P.O. Box 2273, Bartlesville, OK 74005-2273.

ISBN 0-88264-321-5 (pbk) : $5.00

Contents

Preface

Christian Witness Among Muslims was first published by the African Christian Press in 1971.
Shortly thereafter, it was republished in India,
first by the India Evangelical Lutheran Church
and later by the Henry Martyn Institute of Islamic
Studies (Hyderabad). The text at our disposal is a
copy of the seventh printing (1987) by the Henry
Martyn Institute. It has also been translated into
Tamil, Malayalam, Hindi, and Gujarati.

The Preface in the Indian edition notes how
Christian Witness Among Muslims came into existence:

> The author of this handbook has dis-
> cussed Islam and Christianity with thousands
> of Muslims and Christians in various parts of
> Africa, south of the Sahara. These discussions
> have been conducted in English, French, and
> Yoruba, sometimes with reference to the
> Qur'an in Arabic, and sometimes with inter-
> pretation into other African languages.

> As a result, he has written this handbook
> to advise the ordinary Christian how to be a
> better witness for Jesus Christ among his Mus-
> lim neighbors. The material of the book has
> been presented in lectures to Christians com-
> ing from various parts of Africa. Many have
> said that the lectures helped them in their
> approach to the Muslims, and, in return, their
> comments have greatly helped the author.

Why the absence of the author's name? He has preferred to remain anonymous, he says, since so many people have contributed to the existence of this handbook.

And why a North American edition of this handbook? In North America, Islam is no longer a concern for only historians, political scientists, anthropologists, and theologians. Muslims are no longer only across the seas. They are now here also, in our midst, as fellow human beings and fellow citizens, as neighbors, co-workers, and schoolmates. Literally millions of Christians are, or will be, in contact with the 4 to 5 million Muslims on this continent.

Muslims are here. The question is no longer whether or not Christians will respond to them. They must respond, even if only because of the sheer number of Muslims. Rather, the question now is: How shall they respond? Will it be a response of apathy ("Okay, you're here. Just keep your distance from me!") or antipathy ("Muslims are terrorists. I am angry with them and feel threatened by them.")? Or will Christians respond in a Christian manner, viewing Muslims through the eyes of Jesus ("God loves Muslims too!")?

If you are a high school student or a professor or something in between and are looking for a simple, yet profound, guide to help you to relate to Muslims, you have it in your hand. It is especially strong on wholesome Christian attitudes toward the Muslim. As you read it, you might ponder the possibility of giving a copy to your Muslim neighbor to critique and, perhaps, to stimulate his thinking on Muslim-Christian relations.

Publicly and privately, Muslims continue to appeal to North Americans for a better understanding of Islam and for a more charitable treatment of Muslims. *Christian Witness Among Muslims* acknowledges the justification for this appeal and invites Christians to act on it. At the same time, it encourages Muslims also to review their understanding of the Christian faith and their attitudes toward Christians.

Quotations from the Bible are taken from the *New Revised Standard Version.* Quotations from the Qur'an are taken from *The Meaning of the Glorious Koran* by M. M. Pickthall.

We thank Ernest Hahn of Philoxenia/Hospitality Ministry for helping us prepare the North American edition of *Christian Witness Among Muslims.*

May God continue to use this handbook in service to His Kingdom. To Him be the glory!

Klaas Brobbel
The Voice of the Martyrs Inc.—Canada
Mississauga, Ontario
December 1994

Part One

Christian Attitude Toward Muslims

Chapter 1
New Love for Muslims

Whoever does not love does not know God, for
God is love (1 John 4:8).

Right at the beginning, let us confess one of the great failures of Christians. We have not usually shown much love toward Muslims. In olden days some Christians fought wars against them. Fortunately, we now seldom fight with weapons. But some Christians still think it is their duty to battle against Islam with hot argument and abuse. Other Christians live more or less separately from Muslims; they meet on business, but they rarely take one another as close friends.

Why We Should Love Muslims

The main purpose of this chapter is to persuade you, a Christian, to love Muslims. Here are three reasons:

- In many lands, Christians and Muslims live together as members of the same nation, and even as members of the same village or family. Everywhere in the modern world, people of good will are striving for unity and cooperation.

- Jesus Christ said that the second great commandment is: "You shall love your neighbor as yourself" (Mark 12:31). Wherever the Muslim is your neighbor, Jesus tells you to love him.

■ God loves all mankind, including Muslims. He sent Jesus Christ to die for all. So we are called to love Muslims, even if sometimes they seem to be our enemies (Romans 5:6–8; Matthew 5:43–45).

How Shall We Show Love to Muslims?

Be friendly to Muslims. Little by little, try to break down the barriers that separate Muslims and Christians. Start in the ordinary way of greeting and smiling. Pay visits to show your friendliness. Give proper respect. Rejoice with those who rejoice and weep with those who weep. Pray for those in trouble. Be honest in business dealings. If a Muslim has done evil against you, forgive him. If you have done evil to him, ask his forgiveness.

Show your love by cooperating with Muslims for the welfare and progress of your community. Islam and Christianity both call for justice and for compassion toward the sick and needy. There are many things that Muslims and Christians can do together.

Understand Muslims and their faith. Some people think that to be a good Christian you must condemn non-Christians. This is a mistake. (See Luke 6:37.) You are a better Christian if, while holding firm to your own faith, you show love and tolerance in your attitude to people of other religions. Note how charitable Jesus was to the Samaritans (Luke 9:51–55; 10:29–37; 17:11–19) and to the Gentiles (Matthew 8:5–13), both considered enemies by His people.

Sincere Muslims have many things in common with sincere Christians. They are struggling to do good and are tempted by evil. They are sometimes lonely, disappointed, troubled, sick, or facing death. They want to know the meaning of life and seek God as the answer to their problems.

So your love for Muslims means that you first recognize them as fellow human beings. Then, in order to understand them, study the religion that is precious to them. Do not study Islam with the aim of finding fault. Rather, look for its good points and be glad about them.

Tell Muslims about Jesus Christ. Some people misunderstand the word "love." When we say, "Christians should love Muslims," they think we are asking for a sort of compromise. They think "loving Muslims" means: "Don't tell them anything about the Gospel because that might offend them."

That is not what "loving Muslims" means. Loving Muslims means the opposite. When you have something that's valuable, you like to share it with those you love. If we really love Muslims, we shall certainly want to share the wonderful Gospel of Jesus Christ with them.

Further, as Christians we must obey the command of Jesus, who not only told us to love our neighbor, but also told us that "repentance and forgiveness of sins is to be proclaimed in His name to all nations" (Luke 24:47; compare Matthew 28:19,20). There will be more on this subject in Chapter 2.

Summary

This book will help you to understand your Muslim neighbors. It will also advise you on how to explain the Gospel to them. But the most important thing is for Christians to have a new attitude of love toward Muslims. That will be a powerful witness to Jesus Christ!

Two proverbs say: "What love cannot do is not worth doing" and "The person we love, his house is never far away." The Bible says: "And now faith, hope, and love abide, these three; and the greatest of these is love" (1 Corinthians 13:13).

For Discussion Among Christians

- Someone said: "The Muslims of my area are so aggressive and proud. It is impossible for us Christians to love them." How would you answer? (Consider 1 Peter 2:11–16; 3:8–18.)

- Another said: "The Muslims of my area are different from us in race and customs, and we have little to do with them. So we cannot love them." How would you answer? (Consider John 4:7–9,39,40; Acts 10:28,29; Luke 10:29–37.)

- Another Christian said: "In my area Christians and Muslims do love one another. But we are afraid to preach because that might spoil the good relationship." How would you answer? (Consider Matthew 28:19; 2 Corinthians 5:14,15,19,20.)

■ Someone else said: "If we admit the good points in Islam, people will think it is just as good as Christianity. So we had better go on condemning it!" How would you answer? (Consider Matthew 7:1–5; Luke 18:9–14; 1 Corinthians 13:4–6; Romans 5:6–8.)

Prayer

Lord God, our Heavenly Father, we acknowledge that we Christians have not always loved Muslims in the past and present. Forgive us for failing to love our neighbors as ourselves. In Your mercy let Your Holy Spirit kindle within our hearts new attitudes of friendship and understanding for Muslims, for those near us and far away. In the Name of Jesus, Amen.

Chapter 2
Our Message to Muslims

*For we do not proclaim ourselves; we proclaim
Jesus Christ as Lord and ourselves as your slaves
for Jesus' sake* (2 Corinthians 4:5).

First, stop and think. Have you met any Muslims
in the last few days? Have you shown love to
any? Now, we are going to study the above text in
three parts.

We Must Not "Preach Ourselves"

This means we must not have any sense of superiority when we tell people about the Gospel.
"Preaching" does not mean "I am better than
you." "Preaching" means "I have heard some
wonderful news that I would like to share with
you."

"Preaching" does not mean "My religion is
better than your religion." This thought simply
arises from the wrong feeling of superiority. The
Christian preacher may have his private thoughts
about other religions, which should be as gener-
ous as possible. But these private thoughts are no
part of his message, which is simply about God's
revelation in Jesus Christ.

Another kind of "preaching ourselves" is to
be always speaking and never listening. Notice

how Jesus listened to the woman of Samaria and how Philip listened to the Ethiopian (John 4; Acts 8:26–38). Effective Christian pastors listen to their members.

Even more, Christian preachers among Muslims must listen to them to understand their deepest thoughts and feelings. Then when it is their turn to speak, they will be sensitive to their hearers. And their message will be more understandable and attractive.

We Must Preach Jesus Christ as Lord

Do we need to give any message to the Muslims? Some Christians say, "Christianity and Islam are the same—believing in one God. Only the way and manner of worship is different. So there is no need to tell Muslims about the Gospel."

This is a mistake. We are glad the Muslims reject idols and believe in only one God, as we do. We respect the sincere devotion and goodness of many Muslims. But this does not mean their beliefs are the same as ours. Consider the differences:

- Muslims honor Jesus as prophet, but they do not know Him as Lord and Savior. They deny that He is the Son of God.

- Orthodox Muslims say that Jesus did not die on the cross and did not rise from the dead. (See Chapter 7.)

- Muslims seldom call God "Father." They say that God has no sons and people are only His slaves or servants.

So these most precious truths of the Gospel (Jesus as Lord and Savior, His cross and resurrection, God as our Heavenly Father) are seldom, if ever, known to Muslims.

Do you remember the Jews in Jerusalem on the day of Pentecost? They were sincere religious men and women and believers in one God, but God inspired the apostles to proclaim to them Jesus as Lord and Savior. In a similar way, devout and good as many Muslims are, God wants them to hear and believe the great things He has done for the world in Jesus Christ.

"God was in Christ reconciling the world to Himself." But how shall the world know, unless someone tells the Good News? God is "entrusting the message of reconciliation to us." So, unworthy as we are, we are made ambassadors for Christ, appealing to people to be reconciled to God through Him (2 Corinthians 5:19,20).

We Must Be Servants to Those to Whom We Preach

This reminds us again to avoid all sense of superiority. Jesus, our Lord and Master, stooped down to wash people's feet. What will you do in order to be a servant to Muslims? Some Christians may still say, "If we go too far in loving the Muslims, we risk compromising our faith. So we had better keep separate from them." But listen to the apostle Paul: "I have become all things to all people, that I might by all means save some." (Read 1 Corinthians 9:19–23.) Of course, the saying "all things to all men" can be misunderstood. It does not mean, "Worship idols with the idolaters and get drunk with the drunkards"! You must be all things to all men, but you are not to do anything that is against your faith in Christ. You cannot, for the sake of "love," deny Christ!

But apart from compromise, do everything possible to show love, to serve, and to let people know God's salvation through Jesus Christ.

Summary

In approaching people of other religions, there are two mistakes Christians sometimes make. They are either hostile and aggressive, which is forbidden by Jesus' command that we love our neighbor, or they compromise and keep silent about their faith in Christ. Because of love for the neighbor, the Christian must try to present Christ by deed and word to people of other religions.

For Discussion Among Christians

- Someone said, "We must make the Church perfect and unite all the denominations before we can preach to Muslims." How would you answer?

- Have you heard Christians saying that there is no need to tell the Gospel to Muslims? What

reason did they give? Are you now prepared
to answer them?

- How was Jesus "all things to all people" with
the sinners and the Pharisees (Luke 5:29–32;
7:36–48; 19:1–10)? Was this compromise?
What was His aim?

- Deciding how far to go in loving Muslims
without compromising your faith is difficult.
Discuss some examples.

Chapter 3
The Behavior of the Christian Witness

And the Lord's servant must not be quarrelsome but kindly to everyone, an apt teacher, patient, correcting opponents with gentleness. God may perhaps grant that they will repent and come to know the truth (2 Timothy 2:24,25).

In his second letter to Timothy, Paul advises the young preacher how to be a true Christian witness. In the first 13 verses of Chapter 2, Paul tells him to center his faith on Jesus the Messiah, risen from the dead, and to endure hardship for the sake of the Gospel. In verses 19 to 22 Paul warns that everyone who professes Jesus Christ must turn away from evil-doing. Then in verses 24 and 25 (quoted above) he tells how the Lord's servant should behave when he is witnessing for Christ.

"Not Quarrelsome But Kindly to Everyone"

See also verse 14, "Avoid wrangling over words, which does no good but only ruins those who are listening." Often a Christian has set out to witness for Christ but has ended up in a useless argument! How can we avoid this quarrelsomeness?

Avoid attitudes that cause quarrels. Do not aim at a debate in which we are trying to "defeat" the Muslim. Do not argue to prove yourself right and the Muslim wrong. Instead, aim at a friendly discussion in which Christian and Muslim show a sincere interest in each other. Then in this kind way you will seek to bear witness to what God has done for the world in Christ.

Avoid subjects that cause quarrels. Some Christians think they should "preach the Gospel" by attacking Muhammad, criticizing the Qur'an, and condemning the morals of Muslim society. This is a wrong approach. It hardens Muslims against your message and provokes them to reply with criticisms of the Bible and of Christian society.

Avoid situations that may encourage quarrels. Beware of debates that may lead to fruitless contention. Would it be better to have a quiet chat with a few people in private?

"An Apt Teacher"

Understand people. To teach Janice mathematics, you must understand not only mathematics—you must understand Janice also. Study Islam to understand Muslims. Ask sincere questions and listen to the answers.

Go from the known to the unknown. Start with the things Muslims already know: One God; Jesus as prophet, teacher, healer; the last judgment; prayer; and morality. Lead on from there.

Do not start by speaking of the things Muslims find difficult and perhaps offensive (such as the Trinity and Jesus as the Son of God). When you do speak of these, show that you understand the difficulties that Muslims have with these expressions. Say that you want to explain what Christians mean by them. Assure them that we do not believe in three gods, nor in God physically begetting a son.

Go step by step. Keep to one point at a time. If a Muslim mixes many subjects together in his questions, choose the most useful subject and politely ask him to keep the discussion on this one. And come to the others later or on another day.

If you do not know, say so! The Christian need not pretend to be a know-all. If you are asked a question you cannot answer, say that you will try to find out and bring the answer later.

"Patient, Correcting Opponents With Gentleness"

You should not consider all Muslims as opponents! No doubt some will oppose your witness and show their misunderstanding of the Gospel. Then you have to correct them, but with *patience and gentleness.*

Thus you might say, "Excuse me, I have to say something a bit different," or, "I think there is a misunderstanding there." If you meet someone who is bitter or angry, you might say, "Please, we all stand before God. None of us is perfect. Let us not quarrel but sincerely try to serve God and understand one another." Often a smile and a joke will help. Your calmness and patience in a difficult situation may be an impressive witness to Christ.

"God May Perhaps Grant That They Will...Come to Know the Truth"

Some Christians have said, "It is a waste of time, you will never convert Muslims; they will not listen."

Certainly you and I will never convert a Muslim, for conversion is the work of God. Do not imagine that by much arguing you can make someone believe. By too much arguing you may rather provoke people to resist the message.

But we should never set limits on the power of God. He can bring anyone to know the truth. Our task is to give our witness, with prayer and with love, and then to trust that God will do His own work.

In fact, many Muslims are attracted by the Gospel, and not a few have fearlessly declared their faith in Christ. If Christians showed greater sincerity and love, who knows what could happen!

At All Times Pray!

Pray privately for your Muslim friends and their families. Pray for their health and welfare. Pray that God will guide them as they think over your discussion and as they read the Bible; pray that the Holy Spirit will touch their hearts and lead them to the truth.

Pray, too, for yourself, that your love may be genuine and that you will always be learning more of the goodness of God.

For Discussion Among Christians

- In some areas, Christians have difficulty starting a friendly religious discussion. Discuss how to do this.

  You can start by asking a Muslim about his faith, such as the meaning of a ritual or festival. Can you comfort and advise him in suffering or difficulty and so begin to speak of God's love? Can you speak of your regret that Muslims and Christians have so often been hostile or suspicious? Can you offer a portion of Scripture or other Christian writings, saying that you are happy to hear that Muslims too believe in the *Tawrat* (Law of Moses), *Zabur* (Psalms), and *Injil* (Gospel)?

- What passages would you choose when you first ask a Muslim to read the Bible?

- In your experience, is it good for a Christian to offer prayer when he visits with a Muslim? If so, how will you pray?

Part Two

Understanding
Muslims and Helping
Them Understand
the Gospel

Introduction

Part One (Chapters 1 to 3) described the general principles of Christian approach to Muslims. Now in Part Two (Chapters 4 to 12) we introduce you to what you may talk about in your witness among Muslims. Each chapter has five sections:

Understanding the Muslim

This section gives a short introduction to the Muslim point of view on a particular subject. From this you should find out for yourself what your Muslim friends think and feel about the subject.

Steps of Christian Witness

This section suggests how you may lead the Muslim, step by step from what he already knows, to an explanation of the Gospel.

Discussion With a Muslim Friend

This section suggests what to say during your witness. You can discuss the material, encourage your friend to comment, and then respond.

Practical Hints

This section provides practical do's and don'ts that Christians have learned over the years.

For Discussion Among Christians

This section should challenge and inspire us Christians to make sure we believe what we say and practice what we preach.

Wherever possible, Christians should follow the order of these chapters in their discussions with Muslims. Muslims who understand the Christian view of God's unity and love (Chapters 4 and 5) are more prepared to think about Jesus Christ. When they have learned more of the life of Jesus Christ (Chapter 6), they will be in a better position to think about His death and resurrection (Chapters 7 and 8). Once Muslims understand Jesus as "the Word of God" (Chapter 9), they are much more able to make sense of "Son of God," "Trinity," and "Holy Spirit" (Chapters 10 and 11). If Muslims question the authority of the Bible and the reliability of the Biblical manuscripts, look for help in Chapter 12.

Of course, it is often not possible to be systematic. We must be prepared to take up any topic in which our Muslim friend shows interest.

Chapter 4
Love God and
Love Your Neighbor

Jesus answered, "The first is, 'Hear, O Israel: the Lord our God, the Lord is one; you shall love the Lord your God with all your heart, and with all your soul, and with all your mind, and with all your strength' " (Mark 12:29,30).

Understanding the Muslim

Oneness of God. Muslims have a strong belief that there is no god but God. According to Islam the greatest sin people can commit is to worship anything else beside God, that is, to associate (or "join") other gods with God. The purpose of human life is to worship God.

Ritual worship. When they speak of "worshipping God," Muslims think first of the rituals (the ceremonies and outward actions) of prayer, fasting, giving alms, and so on. Yet, if you take the discussion further, many will agree that "worship" includes much more than ritual.

View of Christianity. Because the above two beliefs are so important in Islam (the oneness of God and the performance of ritual worship), many Muslims are puzzled and even distressed about Christianity. They hear that we call on Jesus as Lord. They see that we do not perform anything like their own ritual worship. Do Christians then actually worship one God?

Steps of Christian Witness

The first step in our witness is to reassure Muslims that we believe in one God and are zealous for the worship of God above all other things.

The second step is to share with them the teaching of Jesus that man's "worship" or "service" is, above all, *loving God and loving our neighbors as ourselves.*

Discussion With a Muslim friend

Refer to the Muslim creed: There is no god but Allah and Muhammad is the messenger of Allah. (See Appendix A.) Ask about the use of this in Islam (for example, it is a part of the Muslim call to prayer, and it is spoken in the ear of a new-born child).

Agree that God is one and that man should worship nothing beside Him. Tell how someone asked Jesus Christ which commandment of God is the first and greatest. Ask the Muslim, "What would you say?" Then tell him that Jesus began His reply by saying, "The first is, 'Hear, O Israel: *the Lord our God, the Lord is one*" (Mark 12:29,30).

Yes, it is so important in Christianity that "God is one." Most Christians learn by heart the Ten Commandments that God gave through Moses, which begins with: "I am the Lord your God, who brought you out of the land of Egypt, out of the house of slavery; *you shall have no other gods besides me*" (Exodus 20:2,3).

But what does it really mean to worship only one God? To say it with the lips is not enough. Even Satan knows there is one God. But he does not obey God (James 2:19).

Again, to bow down in a ceremony of worship is good, but it is not enough. People may bow down hypocritically. A proverb says, "Every lizard prostrates; we don't know which one has a belly-ache." Just so, men bow, but God alone sees their hearts; He knows who is sincere in worship.

True worship is to love God and to obey Him, isn't it? When Jesus was telling the first and greatest commandment, He continued: "*and you shall love the Lord your God with all your heart...*" True worship of the one God means to love Him more than anything else, more than we love ourselves, our power, money, or pleasures.

Jesus also told people the second great commandment. Encourage your friend to say what he thinks is the second most important law of God. Jesus said that it is: "*You shall love your neighbor as yourself.*"

Do we love our fellowmen? See how we human beings oppose one another, how we deceive one another, and speak evil of one another! Often even people in one family fight among themselves; how much more people of different towns, people of different tribes, and people of different social classes! Look at us Muslims and Christians: How far have we loved one another?

Yet we have God's command through Jesus to love our neighbor as ourselves. We who are Christians know that we have many faults and have often failed to keep this law. May God have mercy on us all!

Your Muslim friend may like to quote local examples of enmity and jealousy that divide people. As far as possible, do not take sides, and do not judge who is right or who is wrong. Keep to the point that we all are failing to love God and our neighbor, and that we all need God's mercy and guidance to worship Him truly.

Say: "Especially we Muslims and Christians. I hope we may love one another more. Thank you for your kind welcome to me today. Can we meet and discuss this another day?"

Practical Hints

Pray. From time to time during any such discussion, pray silently: "Father, help me to speak and listen in a way that will lead to good understanding between us. Help me to give a sincere Christian witness. Help my friend to hear Your voice in his heart."

Avoid controversy. At this stage, you are not aiming to bring in such controversial questions as the Trinity and the divinity of Christ. But if the Muslim raises them, give a simple, courteous answer, without raising a spirit of debate.

For example, a Muslim might say, "But you Christians are worshipping three gods instead of one." You could reply, "Oh no, please! We wouldn't dare to do so after so many commands to worship God alone. We believe only that the one God has made Himself known to people in three ways: as Creator, as Word, and as Spirit. It is God alone we call upon."

Or, if asked: "Why do you worship Jesus?", answer: "You see, we worship the one and only God through Jesus Christ, because God so wonderfully revealed Himself to us in Jesus. Of course, God is a mystery and it is not easy to explain everything about Him, since He is so great! But, please believe me, Christians can never think that Jesus is a second god besides God!"

Often this short answer will satisfy your Muslim friend for the time being, and you can return to your discussion of love for God and neighbor. However, if he is really eager to discuss the Trinity or the Person of Christ, do not refuse to do so. (See Chapters 9, 10, and 11.)

Use familiar terms. Use names and expressions that are familiar to Muslims. (See Glossary.)

Recommend the Bible. Use the discussion to stir your friend's interest in the Bible. Speak about the Bible reverently, not argumentatively. Offer to lend a Bible or give a Scripture portion. Suggest passages that you know he will enjoy reading, and talk about these next time you meet. Suggestions: Psalm 23; 1 John 4:16–21; James 2:16–21; Luke 10:25–37.

For Discussion Among Christians

- On what occasions do Muslims repeat the Muslim creed? Ask your Muslim friends and find out all you can about what it means to them.

- What can we do as Christians to show that we worship God above all other things?

- Is there any way in which we are failing to love our neighbors as ourselves? How can we put this right?

Prayer

Lord God, our Heavenly Father, You alone are the Creator and Preserver of the whole universe, of the earth, and of all the people living on it. We thank You and praise Your holy Name! Open the hearts of Christians and Muslims that they would learn to live together in harmony and together as Your servants to promote peace on earth among all nations. Encourage and enable us as Christians to share, through word and deed, Your blessed Gospel with Muslims also. In the Name of the Messiah, Amen.

Chapter 5
God, Our Heavenly Father, Is Love

*And the Pharisees and the Scribes were grumbling
and saying: "This fellow (Jesus) welcomes sinners
and eats with them." So he told them this parable:
"Which one of you, having a hundred sheep, and
losing one of them, does not leave the ninety-nine
in the wilderness and go after the one that is lost
until he finds it?"* (Luke 15:2–4; read the
whole chapter.)

Understanding the Muslim

"God is greater!" is repeated in the Muslim Prayer
and in everyday life. After the oneness of God, His
greatness seems to be the most important thing
in the Muslim belief about God. God is far greater
than our thought of Him, greater in power and
wisdom and mercy; nothing is to be compared
with Him.

Does God love all people? This is not so clear in
Islam. On the one hand, the Qur'an calls God
"the Merciful" and "the Loving." On the other
hand, the Qur'an says that God loves the good
people and does not love the bad (Surah 3:134,
140).

Muslims interpret this subject in different
ways. Here we can only say that all Muslims have

some idea of God's love, but not many will think of it in the way that Christians do. The Christian thinks of the love of God as it was revealed in Jesus Christ: "God proves His love for us in that while we still were sinners Christ died for us." This is a strange idea to most Muslims. Only the Bible says that "God is love" (Romans 5:8; 1 John 4:8).

Is God our Father? The Qur'an, the Traditions (Hadith), and the Muslim commentators seldom, if ever, call God "Father." Many Muslims suspect that the "Fatherhood of God" means a physical fatherhood; that is, that God had relations with a woman and produced children. Such an idea is blasphemous to them, as it is to Christians too. Also, many Muslims feel it is bringing God too low if we compare Him with a human being such as a father. However, some Muslims have accepted that they can call God "Heavenly Father" in a spiritual sense and understand themselves to be children of God.

Steps of Christian Witness

The expression "Son of God" often leads to argument. Many Muslims know by heart the verses of the Qur'an that say that God begets no son (Surah 112). It is hard for them even to listen to your explanations. So, do not start your talk with a Muslim by trying to convince him that he is (or could become) a son of God! Instead, start from the love of God, especially as revealed in Jesus. Then lead to Jesus' teaching that God is the lov-

ing Heavenly Father. Tell what it means to you
personally to trust God as Father.

Discussion With a Muslim Friend

The love of God, revealed in Jesus. In the time of Jesus
Christ, people thought that a holy man, a religious leader, ought to have nothing to do with
unholy people. As the proverb says, "A man wear-
ing a white cloth doesn't enter the palm-oil
shop." So people were astonished when they saw
Jesus mixing with despised and sinful people.
They criticized Him for it.

Jesus explained His action by asking them to
think about a good shepherd. A shepherd may
have 99 of his 100 sheep safely at home. But is he
content with that? No, if even one is missing, he
will go out looking until he finds it. Then how
happy he will be when the lost sheep is found
(Luke 15:1–7)!

Through this parable of "The Lost Sheep,"
Jesus was teaching that God is the greatest Shepherd, who loves every one, including the lost and
the sinful. Of course, God's love for sinners does
not mean that He likes them to continue in sin.
His love means that He wants to save them from
sin. For this reason He sent Jesus Christ into the
world to seek and to save the lost (Luke 19:10;
Mark 2:17).

God's love is like a father's love—but far greater.
Jesus went on to show the greatness of God's love
by telling the parable of "The Prodigal Son." (See
Luke 15:11–32, especially through verse 24.)

Many Muslims are drawn to this parable. Find out if your friend has heard it. Show where it is in the Bible.

Discuss the story. When the son was doing evil in the far country, what was the father thinking about him? Did the father still love him? What would you say if the father had rejected him, saying, "Go away; after all the evil you have done, you are no more my son"? Do you think the father should have beaten the boy to punish him? Probably not many fathers would do as this one did, forgiving the son completely and welcoming him back with joy and honor. But Jesus was teaching us that God's love is even far greater than an earthly father's love.

Jesus taught us to pray, saying: "Our Father in heaven…" (Matthew 6:9). But let me make one point clear. Muslims always say that God could not be a father in a physical sense, in the way that human fathers and their wives have children. Of course they are right. Christians agree with Muslims here. We can never think any such thing about God.

When Jesus taught us to call God "Father," it was in the spiritual sense, to show the greatness of God's love. You know that even among men there are some we call "father"; not to say that they physically begot us, but that they care for us and we respect them.

For example, people in India call Mahatma Gandhi "the Father of our nation." Americans talk about their Pilgrim Fathers. Many nations talk about "our Founding Fathers." Much greater than this is the love of God, which Christians think of when we call Him "Father."

The joy of trusting in God as Father. We all have times of trouble; we are tempted by evil and are surrounded by enemies. At such times some people despair of God, thinking that He no longer loves them. If you look at all the suffering in the world, you can begin to wonder: "If God loves us, why does He allow this to happen?"

Yet, through Jesus Christ, we have learned to trust in God's love, no matter what happens. The mighty God, the Judge and the Creator of all worlds, cares for each one of us far more than the best human father cares for his children. His love surrounds us. His love is stronger than all the power of evil (Romans 8:35–39).

In Jesus' own life we see a perfect example of trust in God as Father. Betrayed by friends and tortured by enemies, He prayed, "Father, forgive them; for they do not know what they are doing." Then, at the point of death, He prayed confidently, "Father, into Your hands I commend my spirit" (Luke 23:34–46).

Practical Hints

- If a Muslim raises the question of "sons of God," try to give a brief, friendly answer and then, if possible, return to the main point of your witness. For example: "Of course, we often use the word 'son' as a metaphor or parable, and so the Qur'an speaks of the traveller as 'the son of the road.' We do not mean the road married a wife and begot a child! Similarly, 'sons of God' has a spiritual (not physical) meaning; it shows the great love God has for us and the trust we have in God" (1 John 3:1).

■ Be ready with illustrations of a child's trust in his/her father. For example, a little girl once went out in a boat on the sea for the first time in her life. It happened that her father was the one in charge of the boat. A great storm blew up, people were tossed here and there, many were shouting and weeping. But the little girl sat calm and smiling. Someone asked, "How is it that you are not afraid like the rest?" She replied, "My father is in charge of the boat. He knows I'm here."

Our earthly fathers cannot always protect us, but we know that God is all-powerful. Christians believe the message of Jesus Christ that God is our Father. Through all the storms of life, we know that He is "in charge of the boat" and He cares for each one of us. (In some areas, it would be better to tell this story about a boy. Or tell the story about some other frightening situation, such as being in the jungle at night.)

■ In some languages, the word for "love" may not be appropriate for speaking to Muslims of the love of God. Then you may begin by speaking of God's "mercy."

- Consider also Matthew 5:44,45; 6:25,26,31–33; 7:9–11; Romans 8:14–16; Hebrews 12:5–11.

For Discussion Among Christians

- We Christians say "Our Father," and many of us recite: "I believe in God the Father Almighty." Do we really think about "God as Father" and believe it? What do we do during the troubles of life? Do we trust in the Heavenly Father? Or do we despair, or rely on "magical" protection? Let us get right with God ourselves, so that we shall have a genuine testimony to give to Muslims about the peace and joy of trusting our Father God.

- A good son or daughter is expected to copy the virtues of his or her father. Are we behaving as sons and daughters of the Heavenly Father, showing His goodness in our lives? (For example, see Matthew 5:44, 45.) A proverb says, "The praying mantis has given birth; now it is up to the child to learn to dance like his father!"

Chapter 6
The Life of Jesus Christ

"... preaching peace by Jesus Christ (He is Lord of all)... how God anointed Jesus of Nazareth with the Holy Spirit and with power; how He went about doing good and healing all who were oppressed by the devil, for God was with Him"
(Acts 10:36,38).

Understanding the Muslim

The messengers of God. Muslims believe that God has revealed His will especially by sending messengers to the world. Noah, Ishmael, Moses, Jesus, and Muhammad are called both messenger and prophet. Muslims consider that such persons received Scriptures from God. All preached more or less the same message. At the Last Day they will witness against those who rejected their message.

Muhammad, "the seal of the prophets." Muslims believe that Muhammad received the Qur'an as God's complete and final revelation for all mankind. Also, the life and teaching of Muhammad are believed to give the perfect example for mankind to follow.

A few Muslims do seem to raise Muhammad to superhuman status. Still the orthodox Muslim insists that, however great Muhammad was, he was only a "man, of a purely human nature. He

was neither a great god, nor a small god, he is not
an object of worship; we do not pray to him, but
pray to God for him" (Shaykh M. Abdullah Draz).

Jesus, son of Mary, the Messiah. Jesus is mentioned in some ninety verses of the Qur'an and in
many Traditions. He is called a prophet and messenger, a blessed and righteous one, honored
both on earth and in heaven, one of those close
to God. The Qur'an describes how His birth was
announced by Gabriel to Mary and how she con-
ceived Him miraculously while still a virgin. It says
that He healed the blind and the leper, and
raised the dead. God gave Jesus the *Injil* (Evangel,
Good News) containing guidance and light for all
people. Jesus gathered disciples who believed in
Him as the messenger of God. Many of the children of Israel, especially their religious leaders,
wanted to put Him to death. But God rescued
Him from them. God will place those who follow
Jesus above those who disbelieve, until the day of
resurrection. Muslims honor Him with the titles
"the word of God" and "the spirit of God." (See
Chapter 9.)

Yet, in Muslim belief, Jesus is like the other
human messengers—a created mortal man, no
more than a servant. He must never be called
"God," "Son of God" or "Lord," for there cannot
be any other god or lord besides God. Jesus did
not die on the cross. (See Chapters 7 and 8.)
However highly Muslims honor Jesus, still Muhammad usually remains in their eyes the su-

preme and final messenger of God for all the world.

Steps of Christian Witness

What a problem for us! Muslims honor Jesus in so many ways. Yet, they seem to reject those things that are most important in our own faith: the divinity of Jesus Christ, His death on the cross, and His resurrection. How shall we meet the problem?

As usual, we advise you to go "from the known to the unknown." Do not begin by trying to prove that Jesus is God. A Muslim will almost inevitably misunderstand you and reject what you are saying. Even the disciples did not at first realize that Jesus was God or the Son of God. They had observed His life for many days before Peter was first enlightened to know who Jesus was (Matthew 16:13–17).

So normally your first step of witness about Jesus will be to encourage your friend's interest in the life of Jesus, especially in those events that are also mentioned in the Qur'an. As your friend grows in his understanding of the words and deeds of Jesus, he should see for himself that Jesus is a man and yet more than a man, a great prophet and yet more than a great prophet.

Discussion With a Muslim Friend

We have already seen two very important things in the life of Jesus Christ. In Chapter 4 we saw how Jesus commanded us to love God and to love our neighbor as ourselves. The religious teachers at that time were much concerned about detailed rules and rituals. It was a new and shocking idea when Jesus said that "love" was more important than all these rules.

Then in Chapter 5 we saw how Jesus made friends with sinners and lowly people. In this, He demonstrated to the world how God loves sinners, how He is the Heavenly Father who never stops loving any of His children.

From there we can go on to discuss the events in Jesus' life that the Qur'an mentions:

- Ask your Muslim friend what he knows about the life of Jesus. Ask him to read or listen to the story of the birth of Jesus in Matthew 1:18–25 and Luke 1:26–56; 2:1–40. According to the Qur'an, God says, "We breathed into Mary of Our spirit and made her and her son a sign for (all) peoples" (Surah 21:91).

- The Qur'an recognizes John the Baptist (Yahya) as a prophet and tells the story of his birth. Discuss John and lead to his testimonies to Jesus Christ; for example, "I baptize you with water; but One who is more powerful than I is coming; I am not worthy to untie the thong of His sandals. He will baptize you with the Holy Spirit and fire" (Luke 3:16).

- The Qur'an (Surah 3:49) says that Jesus healed the blind and the leper and raised the dead, but it does not give any details. Most Muslims will be happy to know such stories as Mark 1:40–45 (a leper), Mark 10:46–52 (Bartimaeus), and Luke 7:11–17 (the widow of Nain's son).

Make clear Jesus was not a magician or "wonder-worker," doing miracles to astonish people. His miracles were signs, teaching people about God. They show God's mercy to mankind. They show that in the coming of Jesus "the Kingdom of God is at hand." They call men to repentance.

The prophets had foretold a great day of salvation with a Messiah who would make the blind to see, the lame to walk, the dumb to sing; He would preach good news to the poor and set free those who were oppressed. The miracles of Jesus show that this salvation has come with Jesus Christ (Isaiah 35:5,6; 61:1,2; Luke 4:16–22; 7:18–23; 11:20).

Practical Hints

Do not compromise. Muslims who are friendly to us sometimes propose a compromise: "If you Christians will only leave out 'Son of God,' then Muslims and Christians could agree on one God and Jesus as a prophet. In this way we could end our differences." We do appreciate the good intention of this proposal. But it is impossible for us to omit any part of the Bible's testimony to Christ!

Do not try to prove the Gospel from the Qur'an. Another way in which some Christians have tried to end the differences is to claim that the Qur'an supports vital Christian doctrines that Muslims reject. Thus it is possible, by cleverly twisting the meaning of some verses, to give the impression

that the Qur'an itself "proves" the Trinity, the
divinity of Christ—even that He is Son of God.

But Christians must not misrepresent the
Qur'an. Doing so only annoys Muslims (as we are
annoyed when Muslims misrepresent the Bible)
and it confuses Christians by giving a false impression that the Qur'an and the Bible agree on
Christianity's foundational doctrines.

Do not attack the character of Muhammad. You
are not the judge over Muhammad or anyone else
(Luke 6:37). Attacking Muhammad usually
makes Muslims determined to defend Muhammad at all costs.

Again, be careful about comparing Jesus and
Muhammad, because the comparison usually of-
fends Muslims. They may feel you are doing it to
attack Muhammad, since the position of Jesus
Christ in Christian faith (as Lord and Savior) is
different from the position of Muhammad in Islam (as messenger). Therefore, comparison may
be misleading.

If you have to make any comment on Muhammad, let it be a favorable one; for example, how
he converted an idolatrous people to worship one
God or how he established unity and order
among warring tribes.

*Be careful about what you try to prove from the
miracles of Jesus and His virgin birth.* Some Christians have claimed these as proofs that Jesus is
God or the Son of God.

These "proofs" fail to convince most Muslims,
since other prophets have also performed mir-

acles. Adam also, they may add, came into the world miraculously without a father and mother.

Jesus never used miracles as mere "proofs" of His divinity (Matthew 4:6,7). We advise you to keep close to the Bible witness that the miracles are primarily "signs" of the fulfillment of the prophecy of the coming of God's Kingdom in Jesus Christ and of our need to repent.

For Discussion Among Christians

- Our difficulty may be that we are so weak in understanding the life of Jesus Christ. We know some separate stories about Him. We know John 3:16 by heart. But can we describe His life? Practice giving a five-minute talk about Jesus—not about the doctrines of incarnation and atonement, but simply about what Jesus did and said.

- Give similar talks about some of the Bible stories mentioned in this chapter. In each case, connect the story with a Muslim belief. Tell the story in a lively way. Use the story to show what sort of person Jesus is and how "the Kingdom of God is at hand" in His ministry.

- What special occasions can we use to make the stories of Jesus vivid and personal, both to Muslims and Christians? (For example, when we pray for the sick, we could tell how Jesus healed the sick.)

Chapter 7
The Sacrifice of Jesus Christ

*Jesus said: "The good shepherd lays down his life
for the sheep"* (John 10:11).
*Christ died for our sins in accordance with the
Scriptures* (1 Corinthians 15:3).

Understanding the Muslim

Did Christ die? Many Muslims have heard the story
that God took Jesus to heaven just before the
crucifixion and that God miraculously caused a
substitute to be crucified in His place. They feel
this gives more honor to Jesus than the Christian
belief that He died on the cross. For Muslims, a
crucified Jesus would be a shamefully defeated
Jesus. God would not allow His prophet to die
such a shameful death!

In opposition to this, Muslims of the Ahmadiyya Movement claim that Jesus (not a substitute)
was nailed to the cross, was taken down while still
alive, recovered from His wounds and lived to the
age of 120 years, finally dying in Kashmir.

Thus, in one way or another, most Muslims
doubt that Jesus died on the cross.

Does man need an atoning sacrifice? Muslims
readily admit that they sometimes disobey the
commandments of God. Nevertheless, they feel
that God forgives them their sins because of their
belief in God, their rejection of idols, and their

repentance and other good works. They hope
that on the Day of Judgment, God, who is merciful, will allow them to enter into Paradise. There
is no need, they say, for another to die for their
sins.

Does God need an atonement? Islam emphasizes
the absolute freedom of God. He does whatever
He wills. When He decrees something, He merely
says "Be," and it is. So, if God wants to forgive, He
does not need any atonement. He simply forgives.

Steps of Christian Witness

Thus, Christ's death for our sins, so precious to
us, is puzzling to Muslims. (Remember how difficult it was for Peter to believe that Christ would
die. See Matthew 16:21–23.) So your first step of
witness is, simply, to tell the story of events leading up to the cross. Then let the meaning of
Christ's sacrifice come naturally from the story.

Your witness should balance three aspects of
the crucifixion:

- *What people did:* They opposed Jesus and plot-
ted to kill Him. (Muslims believe this.)

- *What Jesus did:* He made a voluntary, loving
self-sacrifice on behalf of people. (Do Muslims believe He was willing to sacrifice Himself?)

- *What God did:* God so loved the world that He
planned and used the death of Jesus as the
way of bringing forgiveness and cleansing to
humankind.

Discussion With a Muslim Friend

As an introduction, discuss the theme of "self-sacrifice." Find examples from the history or legends of your own people. Or tell the story of Damien: This was in the days when there was no cure for leprosy and lepers were sent away to an island where they lived hungry, dirty, quarrelling, and hopeless lives. Damien, a Christian, went to live with them and cared for them. He eventually caught the disease and finally died of it. He gave his life for them. Go on to tell how Jesus Christ sacrificed Himself for us.

What men did: Jesus brought peace, healing, and forgiveness. He showed men the way to God. You might think that everyone would love Him! But the religious people were angry because Jesus said *love* was more important than their ritual laws. They condemned Him for mixing with sinners. The self-righteous did not like to have their faults revealed, and the powerful men did not like to have their power challenged. Even Jesus' disciples were ready to betray or desert their Master.

The same sins that spoil the world today were the sins that led men to plot to kill Jesus.

What Jesus did: The Messiah could have gone into hiding; instead, He voluntarily set His face to go into the midst of the opposition: the capital city, Jerusalem. As a man, he had natural human feelings and prayed that, if possible, the cup of suffering might be taken away from Him. But His prayer continues, "yet, not my will but Yours be done" (Luke 22:42). He knew in advance that

men would reject and kill Him. Still He would not
allow His disciples to take the sword in His de-
fense and He refused to call on God for a miraculous deliverance (Matthew 26:51–54). He believed that it was God's will for Him to lay down
His life (John 10:17,18).

Why did Jesus the Messiah believe this? Hun-
dreds of years before, the prophet Isaiah had
written his inspired vision of the "Servant of the
Lord," who was to suffer and to lay down His life
for the salvation of people:

> He was wounded for our transgressions,
> crushed for our iniquities;...He poured out
> Himself to death, and was numbered with the
> transgressors; yet He bore the sin of many,
> and made intercession for the transgressors
> (Isaiah 53:5,12).

Jesus saw Himself as the fulfillment of this
prophecy. He foretold that He would suffer and
be killed (Mark 8:31; 14:24). He said that He
came "not to be served but to serve, and to give
His life a ransom for many" (Mark 10:45). He
determined to sacrifice Himself even to death, in
love for humankind and in obedience to God. He
died so that we may live! So the Christian thank-
fully declares that He "loved me and gave Himself
for me" (Galatians 2:20).

What God did: The sacrifice of Jesus is the
supreme sign of God's love for mankind. "God
proves His love for us in that while we still were
sinners, Christ died for us" (Romans 5:8). At the
same time, the sacrifice of Jesus shows God's view

of sin and our absolute need for His forgiveness. So God planned the sacrifice of Jesus for mankind. He made the death of Jesus to be the way for all people to receive His forgiveness, to become His true servants and friends and, yes, to become His children.

Why did God choose this way to save mankind? Could He not have chosen another simpler and easier way? But who are we to tell God what He can or ought to do! Nothing is plainer in the Bible than that God willed the sacrifice of Jesus as His way of redeeming us, redeeming all humankind.

Practical Hints

- We cannot hope to explain fully the meaning of Christ's death. But Christians believe the following:

  - *It puts an end to all other atoning sacrifices.* Man feels his guilt as a stain, a defilement that separates him from God. The children of Israel (and so many people of other religions) have offered animal sacrifices in the hope of cleansing the stain. The Gospel says that it is the sacrifice of Jesus offering His perfect life-blood that once for all cleanses our guilt and brings us into fellowship with God (Hebrews 10:11–25).

  - *It assures us of our forgiveness.* Of course this cleansing from guilt is not automatic. We need to accept it by sincere faith, by trusting in Jesus Christ who died for our sins. So the "way of salvation" is not a matter of first trying to be righteous in order to make ourselves worthy of salvation. It is a matter of first coming as an unworthy sinner and accepting God's free forgiveness (Luke 18:9–14; Romans 5:1–11). What joy to know your sins are forgiven!

☐ *It reveals the horror of sin and the righteousness of God.* Some people might think, "If God's forgiveness is free, we can commit any sin we like. God will easily forgive us!"

In fact, the death of Jesus Christ is a terrible warning against sin. See what humanity's sin did to Jesus! Sin deserves to be judged and punished. But God in His mercy allowed the suffering and judgment to be carried by His beloved Messiah. Through the Messiah crucified, God offers us forgiveness. At the same time He shows us His righteousness (Romans 3:21–26).

☐ *It is the supreme victory.* Christ has won the battle against the powers of evil. (See the next chapter.)

■ The Qur'an says, "They slew him (Jesus) not nor crucified, but it appeared so unto them" (Surah 4:157). Christians find few Quranic verses more difficult to understand than this one. Of all communities, Muslims alone deny the death of Jesus on the cross. Their denial is virtually based on this verse alone.

While wishing to avoid argument, we may ask the Muslims the following questions:

☐ Are you familiar with the Quranic verses that refer to the killing of other prophets (such as Surah 2:61,91; 4:155; 5:70)?

☐ Are you familiar with the Quranic verses that clearly indicate, or easily could be interpreted to indicate, the death of Jesus (19:33; 5:117; 3:55)?

☐ In light of these passages, does Jesus' escape from the cross deprive Him of His full obedience and His total surrender to God?

☐ Does He escape from what He taught His disciples to accept? (See Matthew 16:24, 25.)

You may have to deal with the contention of the Ahmadiyya Movement that Jesus was taken down alive from the cross. This contention falsifies all the evidence of the Bible. The Bible clearly states that Jesus was crucified, that He died on the cross, that He was buried, and that He rose from the dead.

■ Let your main emphasis be on what the Bible says. In telling the story, show how strong is the evidence that Jesus died. (Jesus foretold His death: Mark 10:45; Romans, Jews, and Jesus' disciples were eyewitnesses: Luke 23:47–49; Mark 15:43–45; the grave was sealed and guarded: Matthew 27:65,66). Emphasize the story of Gethsemane, which some Muslims misrepresent by quoting only "remove this cup from me" and omitting "yet, not what I want, but what You want" (Mark 14:36; Matthew 26:39).

Eventually we must show the Muslim how the Bible also links the death of Jesus with the person of Jesus. The people sought to kill Jesus because of the claims He made about Himself (John 10:31–39; 19:7).

■ Both Muslims and Christians refer to Jesus as the Messiah, the Christ. Try to find out what the Qur'an and Muslims understand by the word "Messiah." Compare it with the Biblical and Christian understanding of "Messiah." For Christians, the Messiahship of Jesus and the death of Jesus are inseparably linked.

■ Ask Muslims to tell you about the Great Festival, also called "the Festival of Sacrifice." (See Surah 37:102–107.) Do they perform any sacrifices? If so, what is their significance? Does their idea of "sacrifice" help you to explain to them the sacrifice of Jesus?

For Discussion Among Christians

■ Practice retelling the events leading to the death of Jesus. Include in a balanced way the three aspects of what men did, what Jesus did, and what God did.

■ In language that Muslims would understand, describe what the cross of Jesus means to you.

■ If you meet a person in severe suffering (physical or mental), how will you use the story of Jesus' death to comfort him?

Chapter 8
The Victory of Jesus Christ

Blessed be the God and Father of our Lord Jesus Christ! By His great mercy He has given us a new birth into a living hope through the resurrection of Jesus Christ from the dead (1 Peter 1:3).

Understanding the Muslim

"I take refuge with God from Satan, the accursed" is a daily confession of every faithful Muslim. Through this confession, he recognizes that he needs to be saved from all the powers of evil, within him or outside of him, and that God alone can save him from these evil powers.

Some Muslims (like some Christians) are concerned with created things rather than with the Creator as the way of their salvation. There is little or no Quranic support for the popular Muslim practices of trusting in amulets, the intercession of saints, or even the intercession of Muhammad. On better Quranic authority, Muslims believe that God will save them because of their faith or because of their faith and good works, or simply because God wills to save them.

Yet few Muslims are certain that God will save them now or in eternity. Is this statement harsh and exaggerated? In any case, the best way for Christians to understand the matter is to enquire from Muslims what they understand about it.

Steps of Christian Witness

We need to explain Christ's whole ministry, especially His death and resurrection, as a glorious victory over the powers of evil. Your Muslim friend has likely heard only of the death of Jesus, not of His glorious resurrection and victory over death. "If Christ has not been raised, your faith is futile and you are still in your sins" (1 Corinthians 15:17). Christ lives to intercede for us. Christians "take refuge with God" by trusting in Jesus Christ, alive forevermore.

Discussion With a Muslim Friend

Throughout His life on earth, Jesus suffered temptation from Satan, even as we do. Perhaps you have heard the story of the time when God first called Him to preach. He went into the desert for forty days, fasting and praying, and Satan tempted Him there. Satan took Him up a high mountain and showed Him all the kingdoms of the world in a moment, saying: "To you I will give their glory and authority... If you, then, will worship me..." And Jesus answered him, "It is written, 'Worship the Lord your God and serve only Him'" (Luke 4:5–8).

The following event shows us how Jesus can control the evil forces in people's lives. One day, in the house of God, a man with an evil spirit screamed out at Jesus. Jesus simply spoke His word to drive out the spirit. The people were astonished and said, "What kind of utterance is this? For with authority and power He commands the unclean spirits, and out they come" (Luke 4:31–36).

At last, Satan entered the hearts of men to make them destroy Jesus Christ. Men betrayed Jesus, jeered at Him, and crucified Him. But Satan could not make Jesus do any evil. See how patiently Jesus endured, without anger or sin. Did He curse His enemies? He prayed, "Father, forgive them." He laid down His life, willingly, to save the world according to God's plan. So His death on the cross was no defeat; it was a glorious victory over Satan (Hebrews 2:14,15; 12:2).

Then, to demonstrate the victory, God raised Him from the dead. God has made Christ to be Lord over all the "powers" and "spirits," whether good or evil (Acts 2:36, Romans 14:9; Philippians 2:8–11).

Jesus Christ is alive, with God. He has gone through the sufferings and trials of human life, even through death, for God to make Him our living Savior. When we meet temptation, death, and all the evil works of Satan, we call to the Lord Jesus Christ and He brings us victory. He intercedes with God for us, both now and on the Last Day. If we trust Jesus Christ, nothing can separate us from God's love.

> Who will separate us from the love of Christ? Will hardship, or distress, or persecution, or famine, or nakedness, or peril, or sword?…No, in all these things we are more than conquerors through Him who loved us. For I am convinced that neither death, nor

life, nor angels, nor rulers, nor things present,
nor things to come, nor powers, nor height,
nor depth, nor anything else in all creation,
will be able to separate us from the love of
God in Christ Jesus our Lord. (Romans 8:35–
39; see also Hebrews 2:17,18; 4:15,16).

Practical Hints

■ We are not interested in attacking a Muslim's
understanding of salvation. But we may remind Muslims that their religion tells them to
take refuge in God alone. Moreover we
should testify to the blessing of trusting in
God through Jesus. Because of what God has
done for us through Jesus, our salvation is
dependent upon *God*, not upon our feeble
and imperfect works, no matter how good
they appear to us. *He* is our Refuge and Salvation. And *He* has sent Jesus to be our *way* to
Himself.

■ Christians have several symbols of their faith.
They should learn, as well as help others to
learn, how to use these symbols properly. Two
of these—baptism and the Lord's Supper—
instituted by the Lord Jesus, are to help us
share in God's grace. Let us administer them
in such a way that they will be a strengthening
of the Church's faith and a witness to outsid-
ers (1 Corinthians 11:26). There are other
symbols we can use for our own faith, as well
as for witnessing to others: the Scripture text
on the wall, the Bible displayed in the house,

prayer together in the family; on public occasions, processions and a reverent posture in prayer.

The water, bread, and wine or the paper and ink of a Bible text have no magic power in themselves to help or harm anybody. They are not charms. But as signs they express and deepen our faith in Christ and help us to receive God's salvation, power, and guidance.

Some Christians display a cross or pictures of Jesus Christ as a reminder to trust in Him. We should be clear that we are not worshipping pictures or a cross.

■ Two small points may help a Muslim to believe Christ's death and resurrection. Jesus lived a fully human life; so, it was natural for Him to go through the human experience of death (Hebrews 2:14,15). Secondly, according to the Qur'an, Jesus raised the dead; so, it should not be difficult for Muslims to believe that He Himself could rise from the dead, especially since the Bible so clearly states that He has risen from the dead.

For Discussion Among Christians

■ What factors in Jesus' life did Peter emphasize in his sermons in the Book of Acts? (Compare 1 Corinthians 15:3,4.)

■ Discuss the cross and resurrection of Jesus as the heart of the Gospel. Consider the witness

of Jesus' disciples before and after His resurrection.

- How does the resurrection of Jesus make a
  difference in your life?

- Are you trusting in material things, the things
  of this world? Do you have a sincere testimony
  on this? (See Acts 19:18–20.) Or are you tak-
  ing refuge with God alone, through Jesus
  Christ?

- Do you believe that all evil power can be
  conquered in Christ's name?

- Are we helping one another to overcome
  evil? Happy is the church where James 5:13–
  20 is practiced!

Chapter 9
Jesus, the Word of God

*In the beginning was the Word, and the Word
was with God, and the Word was God... All
things came into being through Him... What has
come into being in Him was life, and the life was
the light of all people... And the Word became
flesh and lived among us... full of grace and
truth* (John 1:1–4,14).

Understanding the Muslim

God is One and Most Great. Remember that the
great sin in Islam is to worship other gods besides
God. Do not be surprised if Muslims are suspicious of your testimony of Jesus Christ, wonder-
ing whether you are making Jesus into a second
god.

Also, although Muslims can think of God as
"near," the main emphasis is that He is far above
us, completely different and separate from people. So if you use such language as "God became
man" or "Jesus is both man and God," Muslims
may feel you are saying something impossible or
meaningless.

God speaks. Islam teaches that God speaks to
man—through angels and prophets. God's Word
accomplishes anything that He wants. Most Muslim theologians say that the Word (*kalam*) of God

is an eternal attribute or quality of God. It was never created, but has come into the world in the form of Holy Scriptures, especially the Qur'an. This is something like the idea of John 1:1, although not exactly the same. Roughly speaking, one can say that Muslims believe: "In the beginning was the Word of God...and the Word became a book."

The Word of God (Kalimat-Ullah). This is a popular Muslim title for Jesus: "God's word which He conveyed unto Mary" (Qur'an 4:171).

Muslims regard Jesus as a created being only. Therefore, they may not regard Jesus as the Word of God in the same way that the Gospel of John understands Jesus to be. Yet, there is a similarity, which makes it easier to use this title of Christ with Muslims.

Steps of Christian Witness

The previous chapters show the uniqueness of Jesus. He lived and died as a man, yet did and said things that made Him different from any other man. Then who is Jesus? We shall agree with Muslims that God speaks to mankind and we shall witness that the eternal Word of God came into the world as a human being, Jesus Christ.

Discussion With a Muslim Friend

I am happy that you already know much about Jesus the Messiah. The Qur'an says He was born of a woman, just as we have been, and "he and his mother both ate food." Yes, the Bible, too, teaches that Jesus lived a real human life among men. He grew up as our children do. He ate and drank and experienced joy, pain, suffering, and temptation—although never falling into sin. He became a great religious teacher and leader. Muslims call Him a messenger and prophet of God.

Yet there is something more about Jesus in the Bible. Things happened in His life that make Him different from any other prophet. These lead us to believe that Jesus was a man, yes, but also more than man.

His miraculous birth was a "sign to all mankind." John the Baptist, himself a prophet, pointed to Jesus as someone far greater than himself. Jesus announced, "The Kingdom of God is at hand." With His coming a new age had dawned.

This new age was the fulfillment of all that God had promised through the prophets of Israel. Through Jesus, blind people received their sight, lepers were healed, the dead were raised to life, sinners were forgiven and converted, and the poor, despised people heard the good news of God's love. Jesus revealed that God is our loving Father. A person's first duty is not to observe many religious rules, but to repent: that is, to turn from evil to God, to love God and love one's neighbor.

Men rejected Jesus Christ. They seized Him and killed Him. But that was not the end. Jesus' death did not mean He was defeated. God made His death to be a sacrifice by which Jesus took

away our sins and gave us peace with God. God
also raised Jesus from the dead in victory over all
the powers of evil. Jesus lives! To those who trust
Him He gives a share in His victory over evil.

After His resurrection, Jesus said these
astonishing words: "All authority in heaven and
on earth has been given to me...And remember,
I am with you always, to the close of the age." On
the Last Day, the Lord Jesus Christ will be the
judge (Matthew 28:18–20). He will tread all evil
under His feet and will fully establish the Kingdom of God the Father (Matthew 25:31–46; 1
Corinthians 15:24–28).

All of this is the clear testimony of our Bible,
setting Jesus on a different level from the rest of
humanity. But the Bible says just as clearly that
God is one and no other is to be worshipped
besides Him. How then shall we describe Jesus?

Many, both Christians and Muslims, have
found the answer in the first verses of John's
Gospel: "In the beginning was the Word, and the
Word was with God, and the Word was God." So
when we read in the Bible about "the Word of
God," it does not mean another thing besides
God. "The Word" means God Himself in action,
God expressing Himself.

The Gospel according to John goes on to
explain who Jesus Christ actually is. The eternal
Word came into the world, was born and lived as
a human being, humbling Himself by coming to
our level, showing us the glory of God and bringing us salvation. "And the Word became flesh

(human being) and lived among us...full of grace and truth" (John 1:14). Jesus the Messiah is the Word of God. This thought is not strange to Muslims.

We should add: We are sorry if we Christians have sometimes given you the false impression that we make Jesus into another god besides God. This is not what we mean. We mean that God's eternal Word came to live a human life among people, as the Messiah Jesus. God so revealed Himself in His Word, Jesus Christ, that we know God as our Heavenly Father and pray to Him "through Jesus Christ our Lord." By believing in Jesus, we put our trust in God. By honoring Jesus, we honor God's Word and we honor God (John 12:44,45).

Practical Hints

■ Take a simple illustration from human speech. Where was my word before it came out of my mouth? You may say it was in my heart or brain. But if I call a doctor to cut open my heart or my head, can he find my word there? It seems, mysteriously, that I and my word are the same and cannot be separated. I am in my word and my word is in me. Whatever my word does (for example, it may please you or annoy you), it is I who am doing it by my word. So whatever the Word of God does, God Himself is doing it.

Apply this to Mark 2:1–12. How could the Son of Man (Jesus) have authority to forgive sins (verses 5,7,10)? How can the Son of Man be judge on the Last Day (Matthew 25:31–33)? This is possible because Jesus is the Word of God. What He does is the action of God Himself.

■ Muslims call Jesus "the spirit of God." We are glad that they want to give Him such honor. But what do they mean by calling Jesus by this name? The Bible clearly states that Jesus is a human being, flesh and blood. It also clearly indicates that God's Spirit was with Jesus and filled Him (Mark 1:1–10; Luke 4:1–19).

■ Do not to jump into controversies about Christian doctrine. First introduce the life and teaching of Jesus, with the prayer that God Himself will show your friends who Jesus is.

When asked the direct question, "Who is this Jesus?", answer in the language of the Bible rather than in the language of Church creeds. The creeds were written to instruct Christians and to warn them against heresies. They are less suitable for explaining the Gospel to non-Christians initially. Moreover, since many Muslims feel that the Bible (especially the Gospel accounts) has authority, they may respect what you say even more, if it is clearly based on the Bible.

Language such as "second person of the Trinity," "being of one substance with the Father," and "divine and human natures of Christ" will seldom help you explain your beliefs to Muslims.

■ So far in these discussions we have presented Christ without once calling Him the Son of God. This does not mean that we are concealing or compromising on Christ's Sonship. (See next chapter.) It simply means that, in love for our friends, we want to start our witness with the language that they will more readily understand.

This is the Biblical method of witnessing! Different books of the New Testament present Christ in different ways. Some books speak repeatedly of Jesus as the Son of God; other books (Acts and Revelation) rarely use the title, and still others use it not at all (Timothy, Titus, 1 Peter).

For Discussion Among Christians

■ Practice telling who Jesus is along the lines of this lesson. For the moment, don't call Him "Son of God" or "God."

■ As we think of the greatness of our Lord Jesus Christ, let us remember His warning: "Not every one who says to me, 'Lord, Lord' will enter the Kingdom of Heaven, but only the one does the will of my Father in heaven" (Matthew 7:21).

Chapter 10
The Son of God and the Trinity

Long ago God spoke to our ancestors in many and various ways by the prophets, but in these last days He has spoken to us by His Son...He is the reflection of God's glory and the exact imprint of God's very being (Hebrews 1:1–3).

Understanding the Muslim

In the view of many Muslims, to say "Son of God" means to believe that God physically begot a child as we humans do. This would be blasphemy. God is so great that, if He wants to create anything, He has no need to come down to human level and take a wife. He simply says "Be," and it is. Many Muslims know and recite Surah 112 of the Qur'an:

Say: He is Allah, the One!
Allah, the eternally Besought of all!
He begetteth not nor was begotten.
And there is none comparable unto Him.

Muslims feel deeply about this. Even if you explain that "Son of God" (referring to Jesus) has nothing to do with physical begetting, many still suspect that somehow this title is dishonoring to God. Some modern Muslims, nevertheless, do accept that Jesus could be called "Son of God" in a spiritual sense. But they say that any righteous person can be called "son of God." Jesus is only one among God's righteous people.

If you tell Muslims that "Jesus is God," they will inevitably misunderstand you. (Do we understand it ourselves?) They may ask, "Do you mean that when Jesus was born, God was born; that when Jesus was (as you say) dead for three days, God was dead? Then, please, who was looking after the world while God was dead?" These are fair questions and hard to answer.

When Muslims criticize the doctrine of the Trinity, they usually have the idea that it means three gods, of whom Allah (God) is only one; or that it means dividing God into three parts.

> They surely disbelieve who say: Lo! Allah is the third of three... (Surah 5:73).

> And when Allah saith: O Jesus, son of Mary! Didst thou say unto mankind: Take me and my mother for two gods beside Allah? (Surah 5:116).

Steps of Christian Witness

First, set your Muslim friend's mind at rest. Trinity = Tri-*unity*. Christians believe in one God, in God's unity. Christians are opposed, as much as Muslims are, to the idea of three gods, or to the idea of God's having a physical son. Then take good-humored examples from everyday life, using these to introduce what the Bible means by "Son of God."

Discussion With a Muslim on the Son of God

Give illustrations to show that, when in everyday speech men say "son of something," they often mean it "spiritually" (as a parable or metaphor) and do not mean physical sonship. Give examples, such as son of the road, sons of thunder, sons of light. Present these in a humorous way, not argumentatively. Emphasize that we speak of Son of God only in a spiritual sense.

Give illustrations from everyday life and from the Bible to show the relationship of son to father (apart from the physical relationship, which is excluded). Find proverbs, stories, and experiences to help make the conversation interesting. Lead to one or more of these points:

- The son is the *picture of his father*. When we know the son, we know what the father is like (Hebrews 1:3; John 14:9).

- The son has the *closest knowledge of his father* and obeys his father (Matthew 11:27; John 8:28,29).

- The son is the *highest representative of his father*. He can stand in the father's place and receive the honor due to his father (Mark 12:1–9).

Show how God told Jesus at His baptism that He was the Son of God (Mark 1:11); it does not mean "physically begotten." Jesus' prayers show how He trusted in God as Father. When Peter recognized Jesus as "Son of God," Jesus congratulated him and said that God Himself had revealed this to Peter (Matthew 16:16,17).

Many Muslims will be partly satisfied by these explanations. Still, because of their tradition, they do not find it easy to give the title "Son of God" to Jesus. You need not argue about it. If your friend finds it easier to think of Jesus as the Word of God or Messiah, be content for him to do so for the present. Trust God to make things clearer in time.

Discussion With a Muslim on the Trinity

Show that Christians are firmly committed to the belief in one God and that nothing is to be worshipped besides Him (Mark 12:29; Exodus 20:2,3).

The Bible shows this one God revealing Himself in three ways: as Father, as Son, and as Spirit. Or, if your Muslim friend is finding it hard to listen to the titles "Father" and "Son," you may say that God reveals Himself as Creator, Word, and Spirit. Also, mention that this does not mean God changed Himself from one thing to another. He always exists as these three.

Of course, God is a mystery, far above our thought. No Christian can explain exactly how God exists in three ways. Neither will a Muslim claim to explain fully the nature of God. But simple examples can help us to think about it.

For example, Mr. So-and-So is a mechanic, a husband, and a church member; you may meet him at work, at home, or in church; all the time he is these three things, yet he is only one man. Similar examples are man, who mysteriously exists as body, mind, and soul; and the sun, which we see as a globe in the sky, as rays in the air, and which we feel as warmth on the body.

Emphasize that your examples are imperfect. Examples do not prove the Trinity; they just help people to think about its meaning.

The doctrine of the Trinity is simply the way Christians try to summarize what the Bible teaches about God, Jesus, and the Holy Spirit. Rightly understood, this doctrine exists to *defend* the unity of God and to guard against the false idea that Jesus is a god besides God.

For example, the Bible says that Jesus does things that no created being could do: He forgives us our sins, He holds all authority in heaven and earth, and He will be the judge on the Last Day. Someone reading this might mistakenly think that Jesus is another god besides God. The doctrine of the Trinity warns us against any such misunderstanding. It is the *one* God who reveals Himself through His Word; this Word lived as a man among humanity, Jesus the Messiah. So what Jesus does is not something apart from God; the acts of Jesus are acts of God Himself.

Likewise, the one God reveals Himself to us as Holy Spirit. God works in us and among us through the Holy Spirit. The acts of the Holy Spirit are acts of God Himself.

Acknowledge that mere talking cannot convince anyone about the Trinity and Son of God. God wants people to trust in Him through Jesus

Christ. When we trust in Christ, little by little we shall understand the doctrines.

Practical Hints

- Do not be annoyed with the Muslim for raising these questions and for not being easily satisfied. They are fair questions.

  Do not refuse to answer by saying, "It is just a mystery." Truly, God is a mystery; nevertheless, He has given us many things in the Bible that people can and should understand. Be prepared to show texts of the Bible (especially from the Gospel accounts) that reveal Jesus as the Son of God. But do not stop there; go on to explain the meaning.

  Do not start a doctrinal debate in which you try to defeat one another. Do not argue. Listen, explain, pray, and leave the conclusion with God.

  Try to keep to one subject at a time. Do not mix up Jesus as God, Jesus as Son of God, and Christians as sons of God.

- If a Muslim points out that other people besides Jesus are called "sons of God," welcome the point. The Israelites as a whole (Hosea 11:1) and Christians, "adopted" through God's mercy (Galatians 4:4–7), are called "sons of God." This means that they are called to know and to obey God and to be His representatives in the world (as discussed earlier in the chapter). But they do this imperfectly; Jesus Christ alone is perfect in His Sonship.

■ Do you believe that Jesus is God? If a Muslim asks this, it is probably best to reply (as in Chapter 9) that Jesus is the eternal Word of God who came into the world and died as a human being. You may answer also in the words of Colossians 1:19,20; 2:9.

Or you could say, "Jesus is God showing Himself to us in this world, communicating as a human being with us as human beings in ways human beings communicate."

The Christian belief that Jesus is God showing Himself to mankind (the incarnation) may be difficult for Muslims to grasp and may even create misunderstandings for them. It does not mean that God lost control of the universe for three days! It does not deny that Jesus lived a real human life, though some Christians may carelessly give that impression. If you say that Jesus is truly God, you should say also that He is truly man. After all, if God's uncreated Word (uncreated like God Himself) can become a created book (the Qur'an) in this world, cannot God's uncreated Word become a created human being (Jesus), if God wills?

■ Some Christians speak much about Jesus— "Jesus saves," "Come to Jesus"—and very little about God. This gives Muslims the impression that we are making Jesus a second god or a substitute for God.

Bible texts emphasize that God sent Jesus and acted in Him (John 17:3; Romans 3:25; 5:8; 2 Corinthians 5:19) and that the work of Jesus is entirely to the glory of God (John 12:27,28; Philippians 2:11; 1 Corinthians 15:28). Study these texts. Practice speaking with emphasis on what God did in Christ and on faith in God through Christ.

For Discussion Among Christians

- Practice speaking among yourselves about the Sonship of Christ in accordance with the suggestions above. Help each other to find good illustrations. Remind yourselves often that you are aiming not to argue about words, but to lead men to Jesus. We, too, need to draw closer to Jesus.

- In the same spirit, practice speaking about the Trinity.

Chapter 11
The Holy Spirit and the Church

Jesus said: "But the Advocate, the Holy Spirit, whom the Father will send in my name, will teach you everything, and remind you of all that I have said to you... He will testify on my behalf... He will prove the world wrong about sin and righteousness and of judgment..." (John 14:26; 15:26; 16:8).

Understanding the Muslim

Muslims usually use the title "Spirit of God" or "Holy Spirit" in a different sense from Christians. They take it to mean a created being, such as the angel Gabriel or Jesus Himself (Qur'an 19:17; 4:171). The divine nature of the Holy Spirit is scarcely, if at all, recognized by Muslims.

Some Muslims claim that Muhammad is the Advocate (Comforter) whom Jesus promised in John 14 through 16. The Qur'an and orthodox Muslim teaching have never said that Muhammad is the Holy Spirit. Still, some modern Muslims do give him this title, since the promised Advocate is called the Holy Spirit.

Muslims think of "Islam" primarily as submission to God, which is expressed by obeying a complete set of rules for ritual worship and daily

behavior. They feel that the Christian religion
ought to have a similar set of rules given by God
through Jesus. They are puzzled that we do not
have a compulsory ritual and law for all Christians.

Steps of Christian Witness
Tell how Jesus the Messiah promised and sent the
Holy Spirit to His disciples. Then show how the
Church is essentially the community of believers
in Christ, united and governed by the Holy Spirit.

Discussion With a Muslim Friend
A Muslim may introduce the idea that Muhammad is the Advocate or the Holy Spirit. You will
have to show, politely, that this is a misunderstanding of the verses in John 14 through 16. The
Advocate of whom Jesus spoke is not a man but
the Spirit, not seen by the world but already dwelling in the disciples of Jesus 500 years before Muhammad was born (John 14:16,17).

Do not aim to prove the Muslim wrong. Instead, aim to witness to the Christian experience
of the work of the Holy Spirit. Alternatively, you
might introduce the subject of the Holy Spirit by
discussing power.

Everyone wants power. Some want to get
power for evil or selfish purposes. You and I want
the power of God to fight against evil, the evil of
the world around us and the evil of our own
hearts.

When Jesus the Messiah was killed by His enemies and buried in the tomb, His disciples were brokenhearted and hopeless. They had no power. Yet, by the mighty power of God, Jesus rose from the dead.

He showed His disciples His hands and feet, saying, "It is I, myself. Touch me, and see; for a ghost does not have flesh and bones as you see that I have" (Luke 24:39). He told the disciples that "repentance and forgiveness of sins is to be proclaimed in His name to all nations...You are witnesses of these things" (Luke 24:47,48).

Those few, simple disciples had no learning and no religious or political authority. How could they preach to all nations? Jesus promised that they would be "clothed with power from on high."

Soon afterwards, on the day called Pentecost, this power came to them. They recognized it as the power of the *Holy Spirit*, that is, the presence of God Himself dwelling in their hearts. They had already known God to some extent. Now God filled their lives with His divine energy. They prayed with power. God answered their prayer with miracles of healing. They were united in a wonderful fellowship of love and joy. They preached fearlessly that all men who repented from sin and believed in the risen Jesus Christ would receive this same Holy Spirit. The number of believers grew rapidly. This was the beginning of the Christian Church. Read with your friend this exciting story in the Acts of the Apostles, especially chapters 2 through 5.

Try to show that the Christian Church is not a group of people who follow the same particular ritual or observe exactly the same laws of daily behavior. It is a fellowship of people who believe in God through Jesus Christ; it is a fellowship created and guided by the Holy Spirit.

Different members of the fellowship are equipped by the Holy Spirit with different gifts, just as the parts of the body have different functions. Some preach, some teach, some have great faith, some have power to heal the sick, some serve, some are administrators, and some speak with tongues. Every believer, great and small, has some gift of the Spirit by which he contributes to the common life of the Church.

Yet there is one gift that *all* believers should have: the power to love (1 Corinthians 12 and 13). The Church should be a fellowship of people who love one another (and love others as well), because God through Christ has so greatly loved us. We should be people who readily forgive one another (and forgive others), because God through Christ has forgiven us (Ephesians 4:32).

Admit to your friend that Christians often fail to live like this. We sinfully shut our hearts to the Holy Spirit. Yet we do experience the Spirit pricking our consciences and guiding us to be more loving and forgiving.

The "fruit" of the Holy Spirit should be seen in the life of the believer: "The fruit of the Spirit is love, joy, peace, patience, kindness, generosity, faithfulness, gentleness, self-control" (Galatians 5:22,23). The same Spirit fights against the evil of our human nature: our immoral and impure actions, idolatry and witchcraft, quarrelling, fighting, jealousy, anger, and selfish ambition, splitting the community into hostile sections, and drunken revelling (Galatians 5:19–21). Those who belong to Jesus Christ try to put to death this side of their nature. The Holy Spirit has given us a new life. Hence we try to live and pray under the guidance of the Spirit (Romans 8:2,11,26).

Practical Hints

- Muslims know that we do not live up to this teaching. Nevertheless, it is part of our witness that, by God's power, we humbly admit our faults and speak of what we are aiming to be.

- Apply Galatians 5:22 to your behavior with Muslims. Are you meeting them with "love, joy, peace, patience, gentleness…?" If not, you are failing.

For Discussion Among Christians

- Which of the "works of the flesh" (Galatians 5:19–21) is the greatest problem in your Christian community? Of which fruit of the Spirit do you especially need to have more? Pray together about it.

- What do you feel is fundamental to the Church and the Christian life? Do you think of the Church mainly as an organization to be administered and a place to go on Sundays? Or do you know it as a living fellowship, where Christians help and encourage one another, where they also reach out to help others outside their fellowship?

- Is the Christian life mainly a set of laws to be obeyed? Or is it, above all, "God's love poured into our hearts through the Holy Spirit"?

Chapter 12
The Integrity of Our Scriptures

Jesus said: "Do not think that I have come to abolish the law or the prophets; I have come not to abolish but to fulfill" (Matthew 5:17).

Understanding the Muslim

The People of the Book and their Scriptures. The Qur'an frequently calls Jews and Christians "the People of the Book." By this name the Qur'an means that God has given them revelations in the form of books through some of their prophets and apostles. Thus the Qur'an mentions the *Tawrah* (Torah) given through Moses, the *Zabur* (Psalms) given through David, and the *Injil* (Evangel, Gospel) given through Jesus. The Qur'an commands Muslims to believe in all revealed books, not only in the Qur'an (Surah 4:136). Why then do Muslims seldom pay attention to these previous Scriptures?

The corruption of the previous Scriptures. Many Muslims believe that, during the course of history, Jews and Christians have changed and corrupted their Scriptures. Today's Scriptures are not trustworthy revelations of God.

The abrogation of the previous Scriptures. Some Muslims say that the Qur'an, as the final revelation of God, has abrogated (replaced) the previous Scriptures. The Qur'an contains everything that is of value in the previous Scriptures. Mankind, therefore, no longer needs the previous Scriptures.

The Injil. A few Muslims believe that the *Injil* is no longer with Christians. According to them the true *Injil*, as given to Jesus, was taken into heaven when Jesus was taken into heaven. What remains with Christians is an untrustworthy collection of writings of the followers of Jesus.

These are some of the reasons Muslims give for rejecting or ignoring the Bible or parts of it. Some Muslim scholars, however, have not been able to accept these reasons. They accept the present Scriptures of the People of the Book as revelations of God, but they suggest that the People of the Book do not interpret their Scriptures correctly.

Steps of Christian Witness

Muslims often refrain from discussing their attitude toward the Bible. They may not want to offend Christians who treasure the Bible. Or they may feel that Christians will not understand their point of view.

When the authority of our Scriptures is discussed, Christians should patiently listen to Muslim claims. At the same time, the Christian should not allow the discussion to degenerate into a Muslim-Christian "battle of the books," an angry debate about whose book is best and why it is the

best. If the discussion seems to be getting no-
where, turn attention to the content of the book.
The content of a book, not a theory about a book,
is, after all, our chief concern.

Discussion With a Muslim Friend

Why these objections? When the Muslim raises his
doubts about the integrity of the Bible, the burden of proof should rest upon him. Gently ask
him why he believes the Bible or parts of it to be
corrupted, abrogated, or taken into heaven.
What is the evidence? Has he merely heard it
from a teacher? Is there any Quranic evidence to
support these claims?

The Quranic testimony to the Injil. It might help
both Muslims and Christians to examine what the
Qur'an says about the Injil:

> ...and We (God) bestowed on him (Je-
> sus) the Gospel (Injil) wherein is guidance
> and a light, confirming that which was (re-
> vealed) before it in the Torah—a guidance
> and an admonition unto those who ward off
> (evil). Let the People of the Gospel judge by
> that which Allah hath revealed therein.
> Whoso judgeth not by that which Allah hath
> revealed; such are evil-livers (Surah 5:46,47).

> And if thou (Muhammad) art in doubt
> concerning that which We reveal unto thee,
> then question those (the People of the Book)
> who read the Scripture (that was) before thee
> (Surah 10:95; see also 3:3,4).

These and many similar passages point to the existence and the value of the Scriptures with the People of the Scriptures. There is no hint that the text of these Scriptures has been corrupted, abrogated, or taken into heaven.

The People of the Scriptures are not "the People of the Corrupted Scriptures." Why should they wish to corrupt their Scriptures? Is it possible that those Muslims who make such claims misrepresent the Qur'an?

The Injil as Jesus' Scriptures. The *Injil* is Jesus' book in the sense that He is the inspiration for these Scriptures and the focal point of their witness.

On the other hand, the Christian may do well to help the Muslim to understand that Jesus never received the *Injil* in the way that Muslims understand the prophets and apostles to have received their Scriptures from God. Jesus Himself is the *Injil*, the Evangel, the Good News. The various writings included in the Scriptures called the *Injil* testify to this.

Whatever your Muslim friend may think of our Scriptures, encourage him to read them!

Practical Hints

The Christian like a farmer. In dealing with such Muslim objections a Christian may be compared to a farmer who clears and ploughs the land before he sows the seed. With the help of the Qur'an, he tries to remove some doubtful ideas about the Bible that Muslims have. (This does not mean that Christians believe the Bible because of the testimony of the Qur'an to the Bible.) With the removal of these false ideas about the Bible, the Muslim may be more ready to receive its message with an unbiased mind and an open heart.

The Christian like a storekeeper. The Christian is like a storekeeper who introduces his customer to a new kind of rice in his shop. He does not ask his customer merely to admire the rice; he suggests that he tests it by tasting it. Thus, the Christian does not only talk about the Bible; he also invites his Muslim friend to taste the sweetness of its Word and experience the goodness of God. What better testimony to the Bible than the Bible's own testimony to itself!

The adamant customer. Even if the Muslim continues to hold his arguments against the integrity of the Bible, invite him to read parts of it so that he at least has some understanding of what he rejects. Someone has said: "The Bible, like Paul in chains, is able to give a worthy testimony to itself."

For Discussion Among Christians

■ Occasionally we read of Christians in some countries who cannot obtain a Bible. If a copy comes to hand, they secretly and laboriously copy it so that others can share its message. Can you imagine you and your congregation without a Bible? Do we sometimes take the Bible for granted, like air or water or sunshine?

- Have you ever shared a Bible or a Gospel portion with your Muslim neighbor? Would he prefer it in English, in another language, or even both? Does your sharing, or failure to share, indicate its value to you?

- Discuss Muslim responses to the Bible that you have heard. How best can you respond? Do you feel that references to the Qur'an can help you encourage your Muslim friend to read the Bible?

- How would you feel if a Muslim corrected you, a Christian, on the basis of the Bible? Would you be grateful to him? Would it be right for you to help him by showing him a passage from the Qur'an that he did not know or had forgotten?

- Have you noticed how carefully Muslims handle the Qur'an? What do they think of Christians who handle the Bible carelessly?

- Consider Jesus' answer to the Sadducees: "Is not this the reason why you are wrong, that you know neither the Scriptures nor the power of God?" (See Mark 12:18–27.)

- Consider the 12-year-old Jesus "in the Temple, sitting among the teachers, listening to them and asking them questions" (Luke 2:41–52). Give other instances when Jesus used or referred to the Scriptures.

Comments From Two Muslim Scholars on the Bible

The famous Egyptian Muslim scholar, Muhammed Abduh, notes with reference to the charge of the corruption of the text of the Bible:

> It would not have been possible for Jews and Christians everywhere to agree on changing the text. Even if those in Arabia had done it, the difference between their books and those of their brothers, let us say in Syria and Europe, would have been obvious. (J. Jomier, *Jesus, the Life of the Messiah*, CLS, Madras, 1974, p. 216.)

Adil Ozdemir, a Turkish Muslim scholar states:

> ...I am talking about us Muslims. There also seems to be a contradiction in our attitude toward the People of Scriptures (Jews and Christians). We respect Jesus but not Christianity. We believe in the Scriptures but refuse to read the Bible. I know that this is a sensitive issue, but it comes to my mind and I cannot help reflecting upon it. In my personal background I was led to believe that there are no more true Christians today who follow Jesus. I was also told that Christians changed their Scripture. If this had been true, then we might have proven how all this happened and why. We should have discussed this point with our Christian friends. (Newsletter No. 34, 1987, Office on Christian-Muslim Relations, NCCC, USA.)

Part Three

Helping the Serious Enquirer

Introduction

In Part Three, the final two chapters of our book, we shall think especially of the Muslims who are interested in the Gospel of Jesus Christ. Perhaps they are thinking of becoming Christians, or perhaps they have already begun to believe in Christ. We shall call this kind of Muslim "the enquirer." What special help does the enquirer need to understand and follow the Christian way?

In these chapters we shall discuss themes in Islam, the same themes in Christianity, and how we can help the enquirer.

Chapter 13
Bible Study and Prayer

They devoted themselves to the apostles' teaching and fellowship, to the breaking of bread and the prayers (Acts 2:42).

Bible Study

Scripture in Islam

The Muslim idea of Scripture, as we have seen, is different from the Christian idea. Therefore, the Muslim enquirer may need special help to know how to study the Bible.

- Muslims believe that the Qur'an is the supreme revelation of God.

- They believe that the Qur'an did not come from the mind of Muhammad. Rather, it is God's eternal Speech sent down from heaven through the angel Gabriel to Muhammad. Many Muslims would say that only the Arabic Qur'an is truly the Qur'an. A translation of it is only an interpretation.

- Islam has codes of law (based primarily on the Qur'an and Traditions) to tell the Muslim exactly how to behave in life and worship. This law is called the *shari'ah*.

- Generally Muslims recite the Qur'an with a different idea from the Christians' idea of

Bible study. (See below.) Their recitation of
the Qur'an, especially in Arabic, is mainly a
way to praise God for sending down His revelation and to express their reverence and obedience. Some study it. They may read the
Qur'an, either in the original Arabic or in a
translation or in both.

The Bible in Christianity

For the Christian, the supreme revelation of God
is not a book but a person—Jesus Christ. He is the
eternal Word of God, the Mediator between man
and God. But to enable us to know about Jesus
Christ, God inspired men, through the Holy
Spirit, to write the Scriptures. These Scriptures
tell not only the story of Jesus' life and teaching,
but also of how God spoke beforehand through
the prophets, through the history of the Children
of Israel, and afterwards through the life and
preaching of the Church.

Christians do not believe that revelation must
be brought "straight down from heaven" without
going through a prophet's mind. Rather, God
guides the whole thinking and experience of people so that what they speak or write will come
through their conscious mind and will be truly a
revelation from God. So Christians believe that
people wrote the Bible by the inspiration of God.
We trust it completely as "the Word of God,"
leading us to believe in Jesus Christ who is (in an
even greater sense) God's eternal Word, God's
self-revelation in this world.

We Christians do not think that the Bible exists mainly to be recited. It is there, carefully translated from its original languages (Hebrew and Greek) into our own languages, to be studied and understood.

As God inspired the writers, so He speaks to its readers, telling them how He created all things, teaching them His will and encouraging them to obey His commandments, warning them of the consequences of disobedience. The Bible gives many examples of God's judgment and mercy. Above all, the whole Bible bears witness to Jesus Christ, how God through Jesus the Messiah has saved us from our sin and given us new and eternal life. Everything in the Bible must be read "in the light of Jesus Christ."

Since Jesus has perfected the Old Testament revelation, there are many rules and rituals in the Old Testament (such as circumcision) that His disciples need not obey.

Helping the Enquirer

The enquirer may need your help to understand what the Bible means to Christians. Many things that you may have known from childhood will be strange and new to him. Please spend time reading the Bible with him. Explain the significance of the Bible for Christians. Lend him an introductory Bible study book. Perhaps enroll him in a Bible correspondence course. Let him see the Bible being treated reverently by Christians.

Prayer

Ritual Prayer in Islam

The Muslim Prayer is a ritual that must be performed exactly, in Arabic, before God. To know the meaning of the words may seem to be less important; the important thing is to perform it correctly.

This does not mean (as some Christians may think) that the Prayer is insincere or just an outward form. The reverence and the participation of the whole congregation can be very impressive. We are only pointing out that this idea of prayer is different from the Christian idea.

On the other hand, Muslims may also pray in a more personal and informal manner to God, bringing their needs before Him.

Find out from your Muslim friend more about the content of his prayer. Does it include thanksgiving, confession of sins, intercession for others and for oneself? Ask him what his prayer means to him.

Women should observe the ritual laws as men do. Some mosques have a place for women. Usually they pray in their homes.

Prayer and Worship in Christianity

Christians do not think of prayer primarily as "performing a ritual." They think of it more as a conversation with God. We hear God's Word in the Bible and we reply by our prayers and our everyday obedience. We speak in any language we know. We may use set words, or simply open our hearts and speak as a child speaks to his father.

This Christian way of prayer is distinct in that it is offered in the name of Jesus Christ—that is, we dare to approach God as our Heavenly Father because God has first approached us, revealing His love in Jesus Christ. We speak to God because we know that He loves us and seeks our good. We do not pray to "make use of God" for our selfish reasons; we pray that God may make use of us and make us useful to others!

In our prayer we express:

- Our *gratitude and praise* ("Thank You, God!") for who He is and what He has done for us, for everything that each day brings, for all God's gifts of health and material blessings as well as the love of friends (Psalm 103).

- Our *penitence* ("Forgive me, God!") for being evil, for all evil thoughts, for all actions that may have harmed someone (1 John 1:8,9).

- Our *petition and intercession* ("Please, God!") spreading out our wants before our Lord, as a child tells his father and mother how he is and what he needs (Matthew 7:7–11). We add, "if it be Your will," because God knows best what is good for us.

Women have a full share in Christian worship and fellowship. Often the Christian women are more prayerful and energetic than the men!

Helping the Enquirer

The informality of Christian prayer can surprise Muslims, but it can also attract. One former Muslim became interested in the Gospel on the day he first heard Christian *extempore* prayer (a personal, informal, heartfelt prayer). Explain the meaning and manner of Christian prayer. Invite the enquirer to join you in your family prayer, in prayer for others as well as for yourselves, even in visiting and praying for the sick, and so on.

There is also more formal worship in Christianity. The enquirer may be interested in this because it is closer to his experience in Islam. Tell him what you "recite" in your church. It may be the Lord's Prayer, the Psalms, or confession of sin. Everyone joins in singing hymns to express our unity and joy in worship. The Lord's Supper (Holy Communion) will be interesting to many Muslims because it is a sort of "ritual" performed in obedience to the command of Jesus (1 Corinthians 11:23–26). Emphasize that in this service (as in all our worship) we celebrate God's victory through the risen Christ, the One who gives us pardon and victory and who is the living Way to God. We worship on Sunday because on Sunday Jesus rose from the dead!

For Discussion Among Christians

■ If a Muslim attended your church during a Sunday worship service, what would that Muslim find? Would he find what he is accustomed to in Islam: great reverence; much praise to God; proclamation of God's one-ness; everyone participating in the worship? Would he find the things that are lacking in Islam: an emphasis on understanding the Scriptures and the worship; a sense of personal conversation with our Heavenly Father; earnest intercession for the needs of others; joy in the great saving acts of God? Or will he find the preacher giving a monologue over the heads of an inattentive congregation; un-intelligent mumbling of lessons and prayers; a sermon, perhaps unprepared, full of moral-izing but omitting to proclaim God's judg-ment and mercy in Christ?

■ Consider in which Christian gathering your Muslim friend may feel more comfortable, more "at home." Could it be in your home?

■ A Christian wrote a book entitled *Instrument and Purpose*. He intended to show how we should be God's instrument for God's pur-poses. Do we, however, sometimes reverse the roles by wanting (consciously or uncon-sciously) God to be our instrument for our purposes?

■ Some Christians fast, linking fasting espe-cially with prayer. Muslims, of course, are to fast during the month of Ramadan. Can you compare the fasting of Muslims and Chris-tians, noting also why they fast and their ways of fasting?

Chapter 14
Joining the Church

> "Brothers, what should we do?"... "Repent, and
> be baptized every one of you in the name of Jesus
> Christ so that your sins may be forgiven; and you
> will receive the gift of the Holy Spirit"... And day
> by day the Lord added to their number those who
> were being saved (Acts 2:37,38,47).

The Community in Islam

The meaning of being a Muslim. "Being a Muslim"
means that not only does one hold particular
beliefs or doctrines, but also that one belongs to
a certain community. In this community, Islamic
law governs (more or less) the worship, the belief,
the customs, and the habits of the people. Generally, everyone adopts a certain style of politeness
and cleanliness, everyone has an Arabic name,
everyone joins in the fasts and festivals, and often
everyone wears the same style of clothes. All these
things show the solidarity of the community.

The horror of apostasy. The community may be
shocked when a member leaves Islam to join
another religion. They will not feel that the person has made only a private decision of faith;
rather, they feel that he has become a sort of
"traitor" who has gone over to another community, perhaps even a rival community. Orthodox
Muslim law says that an apostate (a convert from

Islam) should be killed—though some schools of Muslim law would exclude the execution of a woman. This is not always done today. Still, officially or unofficially, the apostate is usually persecuted, driven out, shunned, or at least ridiculed. (In the past, Christians often severely persecuted apostates and heretics.)

The growth of tolerance. At the same time, there has been a more recent tradition of tolerance in Islam. The Qur'an says, "There is no compulsion in religion" (Surah 2:256). In some passages, it also pays great respect to the religions of "the People of the Book" (Jews and Christians). Some passages, however, severely criticize the Jews and Christians, especially the Jews.

Nearly all Muslim nations have accepted the United Nations Charter, which declares freedom for individuals to change their religious belief. Many Muslim communities, however, do not grant this freedom to their members. Some Muslim nations have prepared their own declaration of human rights, based on Islamic principles. In fact, the whole issue of freedom of religion, including the correct interpretation of Qur'an 2:256 (it excludes Muslims having freedom to leave Islam, many Muslims say) is seriously disputed among Muslims.

Fellowship in Christianity

The meaning of being a Christian. Ask a group of people what "being a Christian" means and you will get interesting answers. Some will think being a Christian means going to church or even following Western customs. Others will say it means being loving and kind. Certainly a Christian should go to church and should be loving, but the essential meaning of being a Christian is twofold:

- To have *personal trust* in God through the Lord Jesus Christ
- To have *fellowship* with others who share a similar trust

This definition warns us against three common misunderstandings of Christianity: formalism, individualism, and perfectionism:

- *Formalism:* Relying too much on the outward form. To be a Christian is not to be born into a certain community, or to follow certain customs and laws, or even to perform a certain religious ritual. No! Being a Christian means having a personal trust in God through Christ.

- *Individualism:* Thinking that faith is merely an individual thing, "just between you and God," and that there is no need for a Christian to join a church fellowship. Faith is certainly personal, but it is also something that you should have in fellowship with other believers. To be "born again" is also to be born into a family! A Christian is a member of the Body of Christ. "We declare to you what we have seen and heard so that you also may have fellowship with us" (1 John 1:3; see also Mark 3:33–35; 1 Corinthians 12:27; and Ephesians 2:13–19).

■ *Perfectionism.* Thinking that a person is not a
Christian until he or she is perfect in knowledge of Christian doctrine, perfect in obedience to church rules, and perfect in
overcoming all sins. No! Those who put their
trust in God through Christ are at once Christians; they have entered the fellowship and
the new life in Christ. Their understanding of
Christianity may be weak and their morality
may still be doubtful. But our Gospel is of
God's grace for sinners. We must trust that by
God's grace (with the help of the Christian
fellowship also) we will grow in knowledge
and in Christian character. (See Ephesians
2:8–10; Romans 5:8; 14:1,10–13; Galatians
6:1,2; Matthew 13:24–30.)

The loving fellowship. Jesus said, "By this everyone will know that you are my disciples, if you
have love for one another" (John 13:35). Paul
explains further: "As God's chosen ones, holy and
beloved, clothe yourselves with compassion, kindness, humility, meekness, and patience. Bear with
one another and, if anyone has a complaint
against another, forgive each other; just as the
Lord has forgiven you, so you also must forgive"
(Colossians 3:12,13).

The outreaching fellowship. The Church sometimes makes the mistake of hiding away from the
world in order to preserve its power, its customs,
or its purity, for fear of being "contaminated."
The Church sometimes adopts a particular cul-
ture of discipline as a sort of "wall" to defend itself

from the world. We know there are real dangers and problems for Christians in mixing with the world, including the Muslim world. Nevertheless, the Church must reach out in service and in witness. Jesus said, "Go therefore and make disciples" (Matthew 28:19). He said, "I am not asking You to take them (the disciples) out of this world, but I ask You to protect them from the evil one...As You have sent me into the world, so I have sent them into the world" (John 17:15,18).

Helping the Enquirer

Build bridges of love. Try to break down the feeling that Muslims and Christians are two hostile communities sharply separated in dress, custom, and place of residence. We are to love our neighbor. In this way the Muslims will come to respect some Christians as friendly and godly people. Then they will more likely be tolerant toward any Muslim who shows interest in the Gospel.

Emphasize sincerity. Let devout Muslims know that, even though you do not share their belief, you respect their sincerity. Discuss with them the fact that God is not pleased with people who profess a religion insincerely. This may lead to the following thought: If we compel a person to profess what he does not really believe, we are forcing him to act insincerely or hypocritically. There should not be compulsion in religion.

Also, to your enquirer, emphasize sincerity. Let him know that you are not trying to get converts at any price. You are presenting the Gospel in the hope that people will freely and sincerely put their trust in Christ.

Love the enquirer. Inspire other Christians to love the Muslim as well. The previous Bishop of the Anglican Church in Iran, himself a convert from Islam, said, "Most Muslims I know who have followed Christ have done so because of the sacrificial life and sustained love of some Christian friend." To love Muslims means to:

- *Understand Muslims.* Put yourself in their shoes. Think about the way their Muslim community may be putting pressure on them. Do not expect them to be perfect Christians right away.

- *Pray for Muslims.* And pray with them. Visit them and give them a warm welcome to your home as well as to worship. If the church services are not held in their language, try to have a group (however small) worship in their language.

- *Help Muslims.* But help them in such a way that you do not destroy their independence. If a Muslim has lost his job or property through his conversion, help him to become self-reliant again. Where a former Muslim is employed by a church or mission, let it be work that gives the new convert as much responsibility and respect as possible. Such matters should be handled in close consultation with local Christians.

Teach the enquirer. Help enquirers to understand Christian belief and practice in order that they may grow in personal faith and, at the same time, be able to answer questions and criticisms from other Muslims. Go through the teaching of this book, especially the sections "Discussion With a Muslim Friend" in Chapters 4 through 12. Explain the place of fellowship in Christian faith. Tell him that the Church is made up of pardoned sinners and not of perfect saints. This may encourage him to feel he can join and will warn him not to be too disappointed at what he finds there. Prepare him to witness and to face difficulties, even possible persecution (Matthew 5:11,12; Mark 8:31–38; 1 Peter 2:9,19–25).

Need it be added that preferably a female instructs a female and a male instructs a male?

About Baptism and Profession of Faith

Both the enquirer and his Christian friends must earnestly seek the guidance of the Holy Spirit about the time for open profession of faith and baptism. The enquirer, of course, should make the decision.

It is a normal and needful part of the Christian life to declare one's faith openly and to be baptized. The "secret believer" who tells no one of his faith is missing some of the greatest riches of the Christian life. The believer who professes his faith without being baptized may be in a "safer" position, but still misses a great blessing. Nevertheless, we have to look sympathetically at the practical difficulties.

It would usually be wrong to baptize a minor without the consent of his or her parents. Decision at the age of majority, when the youth can act independently, depends on the outlook of the society.

Most Muslim societies regard a woman (at least a young woman) as a dependent in the same sense that a child is. It will generally do more harm than good to baptize her without the consent of parents or husband. If a woman is to be baptized, the greatest care must be taken to do it honorably and to give her the support of the Christian fellowship.

Where an adult Muslim male puts his trust in Christ, he should be helped to see from the Bible the value of profession of faith and baptism. It should be expected that the Holy Spirit will lead him to an earnest desire to take these steps.

On the other hand, it is understandable that such a man may wish to become well-grounded in the faith and Bible knowledge before exposing himself to the criticism and perhaps persecution of his fellows. He may want to become financially independent first. Or he may also wish to postpone his baptism for a year or two so that he can witness in his Muslim society instead of being cast out at once. Thus he might win his family and some friends to be baptized as a group. Or at the least the Muslims might come to tolerate his conversion.

Nevertheless, there is a tremendous danger in such postponement. Cut off from Christian fellowship and without the challenge of witnessing, the new convert's faith may weaken. After a certain point it is usually better for new believers to be baptized and to join the Church, even if this means they must be cut off from Muslim society.

We must prayerfully rely on the Holy Spirit to indicate to the converts themselves when that right time is. Christians must surround the enquirers with love and fellowship both before and after their open confession and baptism. At their baptism, there should be Christian sponsors who take special responsibility to guide and encourage them.

A Prayer

O God, pour out Your blessing on the peoples of Islam.

Grant that these, who always proclaim Your greatness, may know the greatness of Your love revealed in Jesus the Messiah.

Forgive us that so little of Your love has reached the Muslims through us.

Take away from us our pride and our coldness.

Teach us to love our Muslim neighbor as ourselves.

Help us to understand them and to help them understand Your Gospel.

And if any of us should suffer at the hands of Muslims, teach us to overcome evil with good, through Jesus Christ our Lord. Amen.

For more information regarding literature about Islam and Muslims and literature for Muslims, please contact:

Fellowship of Faith
P.O. Box 65214
Toronto, Ontario
Canada
M4K 3Z2

Appendix A
An Outline of Islam

Its Origin

"Islam" means "submission to the will of God." A Muslim is one who submits to God. So, in a sense, all the prophets proclaiming one God, and their followers, have been Muslims. But in everyday speech a "Muslim" means one who submits to the will of God as revealed in the Qur'an and the Hadith, and who accepts Muhammad as the Messenger of God.

Muhammad was born at Mecca (in what is today Saudi Arabia) about 570 A.D. In this part of Arabia most people were idolaters. However, there were some Jews and Christians, and even the idolaters believed in the supreme God, Allah.

From about 610 A.D. Muhammad began to receive, as he believed, revelations sent down from Allah through the angel Gabriel. These revelations continued from time to time for about the next 23 years and were eventually gathered together to form the Qur'an. Muhammad began to preach that man must give thanks to Allah for all things, worship nothing besides Him, and do good in preparation for the Last Judgment.

A small community of believers gathered around Muhammad, but they were persecuted by the Meccans. So, in 622 A.D., Muhammad, with his followers, emigrated to Medina. Here he was no longer only leader of a religious minority, but became the ruler of a city.

His revelations now laid down rules for the whole life of the community: not only its religious ritual, but also the laws of marriage, commerce, and warfare; the administration of justice; and the rules of courtesy.

More and more Arabian tribes accepted Islam as their religion and Muhammad as ruler until, in 630 A.D., even the Meccans submitted. In 632 A.D. Muhammad led the pilgrimage to Mecca, preached his "farewell sermon," and died soon after.

Islam spread rapidly. Within 100 years of Muhammad's death, Islam had spread throughout the whole of North Africa and extended to the borders of India. In 1994, about one-fifth of the world's population is Muslim.

Its Practice

Islam is derived especially from the Qur'an (the Word of God, according to the Muslims) and the Hadith (the inspired reports of the words and deeds of Muhammad especially, according to Muslims). The following extracts of Muslim origin give a little idea of Muslim beliefs and practices:

The Pillars of Muslim Practice

The messenger of God (blessing and peace upon him) said: Islam is built upon five pillars:

1. Confession: Bearing witness that there is no God but Allah and that Muhammad is the Messenger of Allah

2. Prayer: Performing the ritual prayer

3. Alms: Paying the ritual alms

4. Fasting: The fast in Ramadan

5. Pilgrimage: Pilgrimage to the House in Mecca (*Ka'bah*) for whoever can perform it

The Articles of Muslim Belief

1. Allah

2. His angels

3. His Scriptures

4. His messengers

5. The Day of Resurrection and Judgment

Some Muslims have added:

6. Destiny: The decreeing of good and evil by Allah Most High

Muslim Morality

Some of Muhammad's first followers in Mecca fled to Ethiopia, where the Christian king treated them kindly. This is how they explained Islam to him according to a Muslim source:

O King, we were an uncivilized people, worshipping idols, eating corpses, breaking ties of kinship, failing in our duty toward those under our protection, the strong among us devouring the weak. Thus we were until Allah sent to us a messenger. He summoned us to acknowledge God's Unity and to worship Him and to renounce the stones and images that we and our fathers formerly worshipped. He commanded us to speak the truth, to be faithful, to respect ties of kinship, to treat well those under our protection and to refrain from crimes and bloodshed.

He forbade us to commit abominations, tell lies, devour the property of orphans, or slander chaste women. He commanded us to worship Allah alone and not to associate anything with Him, and he gave us orders about prayer, almsgiving, and fasting. So we trusted him, believed in him, and followed that which he brought from Allah.

Thereupon our people persecuted us. So we emigrated to your country, having chosen you above all others, hoping that near you we shall not be unjustly treated, O King.

Muslim Prayer

The opening Surah of the Qur'an, called *Fatihah*, recited at every prayer time:

Praise be to Allah, Lord of the Worlds,
The Beneficent, the Merciful.
Owner of the Day of Judgment,
Thee (alone) we worship; Thee (alone) we ask for help.

Show us the straight path,
The path of those whom Thou hast favored;
Not (the path) of those who earn Thine anger
nor of those who go astray.

Surah 2, some concluding verses:

Unto Allah (belongeth) whatsoever is in
the heavens and whatsoever is in the earth;
and whether ye make known what is in your
minds or hide it, Allah will bring you to ac-
count for it. He will forgive whom He will and
He will punish whom He will. Allah is able to
do all things...

Allah tasketh not a soul beyond its scope.
For it (is only) that which it hath earned, and
against it (only) that which it hath deserved.
Our Lord! Condemn us not if we forget, or
miss the mark! Our Lord! Lay not on us such
a burden as Thou didst lay on those before us!
Our Lord! Impose not on us that which we
have not the strength to bear! Pardon us,
absolve us, and have mercy on us, Thou, our
Protector, and give us victory over the disbe-
lieving folk.

Appendix B
Muslim and Christian Intermarriage

These days, more young people are mingling with others of different faiths and are deciding for themselves whom to marry. Not surprisingly, Muslims and Christians meet and are attracted to one another. Both Muslim and Christian, if they are Muslim or Christian in more than name only, should carefully consider the implications of Muslim-Christian intermarriage before betrothal and marriage.

According to Muslim law, a Muslim man may marry a Christian or Jewish woman, since both Jews and Christians are People of the Scriptures. A Muslim woman, however, may marry only a Muslim man. The Christian or Jewish woman who marries a Muslim man may retain her faith. But, in many cases, such women are pressured to become Muslims. The children of such marriages must be brought up as Muslims.

In many Muslim areas, Muslim men have only one wife. Some Muslims openly prefer monogamy, condemn polygamy, and dislike divorce. Yet Muslim law allows a Muslim man to have four wives. According to Muslim law, a Muslim man may easily divorce his wife, but a wife may not divorce her husband so easily.

If a Muslim and a Christian truly love each other and truly respect each other's faith as far as possible, they should help each other to be aware of the above facts. It is not enough to blindly love one another and to be unaware of the relative Muslim and Christian conceptions of men, women, marriage, divorce, family life, and society in general, or to blindly believe that all problems can be amicably worked out and settled after marriage.

Muslim marriage is essentially a contract. Christian marriage is a lifelong covenant.

Appendix C
A Glossary of Islamic Terms

Practices

Kalimah	The Muslim Confession that there is no god but God (Allah) and Muhammad is His prophet
Salat or *Namaz*	Ritual prayer
Sawm or *Roza*	Fasting
Zakat	Legal alms
Hajj	Pilgrimage to Mecca

Special Days and Festivals

Ramadan	The month of fasting
'Id al-Fitr	The festival of the breaking of the fast
'Id al-Adha	The festival commemorating Abraham's readiness to sacrifice his son
Muharram	The month in which the martyrdom of Hasan and Husayn, grandsons of Muhammad, are especially remembered

Some Prophets and Messengers

Aiyub	Job
Dawud	David
Harun	Aaron
Ibrahim	Abraham
Ilyas	Elijah
Isa al-Masih	Jesus Christ
Musa	Moses

Nuh	Noah
Yahya	John the Baptist
Yunus	Jonah

Sacred Scriptures

Tawrah	Torah, the Pentateuch, the Old Testament
Zabur	Psalms
Injil	Evangel, New Testament
Ahl al-Kitab	People of the Book (Jews and Christians)
Ayah	A revelation, sign, or verse of the Qur'an
Surah	A revelation or chapter of the Qur'an

Other

Ahmadiyya	An unorthodox (sometimes banned) Muslim sect
Bismi'llah	"In the name of Allah"; an invocation
Khalifah	The successor to Muhammad, ruler of Islam; caliph
Du'a	Free prayer
Din	Religion, judgment
Fatihah	The first Surah in the Qur'an
Hadith	Canonical Tradition
Iblis	The devil
Ilham	Inspiration
Imam	Prayer leader; special leader of Shi'ah Muslims
Iman	Faith, belief
Jahannam	Hell
Jannah	Garden, heaven
Jibra'il	Gabriel

Kafir	One who is guilty of *kufr* (unbelief, blasphemy)
Kitab	Book
Malak	Angel
Mushrik	One who is guilty of *shirk* (idolatry, polytheism)
Nabi	Prophet
Rasul	Messenger, apostle
Shahadah	The confession of Muslim creed
Shari'ah	The religious law
Shi'ah	The major split in Islam, originally political
Sufi	A Muslim mystic
Sunni	The main division of Islam; a follower of the *sunna* (path) of Muhammad
Tawhid	The unity (oneness) of God
'Ulama'	Muslim scholars
Ummah	Muslim community
Wahi	Inspiration